BEYOND BITCOIN

Beyond Bitcoin

The Economics of Digital Currencies

Hanna Halaburda and Miklos Sarvary

First published 2016 by
PALGRAVE MACMILLAN

The authors have asserted their rights to be identified as the authors of this work in accordance with the Copyright, Designs and Patents Act 1988.

Palgrave Macmillan in the UK is an imprint of Macmillan Publishers Limited, registered in England, company number 785998, of Houndmills, Basingstoke, Hampshire, RG21 6XS.

Palgrave Macmillan in the US is a division of Nature America, Inc., One New York Plaza, Suite 4500, New York, NY 10004-1562.

Palgrave Macmillan is the global academic imprint of the above companies and has companies and representatives throughout the world.

Hardback ISBN: 978-1-137-50641-2
E-PUB ISBN: 978-1-137-50643-6
E-PDF ISBN: 978-1-137-50642-9
DOI: 10.1057/9781137506429

Distribution in the UK, Europe and the rest of the world is by Palgrave Macmillan®, a division of Macmillan Publishers Limited, registered in England, company number 785998, of Houndmills, Basingstoke, Hampshire RG21 6XS.

Library of Congress Cataloging-in-Publication Data

Halaburda, Hanna.
    Beyond bitcoin : the economics of digital currencies / Hanna Halaburda and Miklos Sarvary.
        pages cm
    Includes bibliographical references and index.
    ISBN 978-1-137-50641-2 (hardback : alk. paper)   1. Electronic funds transfers.   2. Bitcoin.   3. Foreign exchange.   I. Sarvary, M. (Miklos) II. Title.
    HG1710.H275 2015
    332.40285'4678—dc23
                                                                    2015021525

A catalogue record for the book is available from the British Library.

CONTENTS

LIST OF TABLES

Chapter 1

Introduction

In the last two decades, the Internet combined with the smartphone revolution has created a permanently connected world transcending national borders, time differences, and geographic distance. In this way, the Internet has become the backbone for most of our activities—not only communication and entertainment, but also economic activities, like commerce or work. By the 2010s, it has become actually difficult—if not impossible—to live without using the Internet one way or another.

The technological progress also affected how we store our money and how we pay for the goods and services we need. Most intriguing is that we are changing our perception of what money is, or can be, and are starting to experiment with types of money that have not been seen before in human history—digital currencies. The digital currencies only live in the virtual world of the Internet, computers, or smartphones. They have strange-sounding names, they are governed by often unfamiliar rules, and they require us to adopt new habits if we want to use them. Some of the digital currencies come from issuers we are familiar with, for example, social networks such as

Facebook or commerce platforms such as Amazon. Others belong to the mysterious group of cryptocurrencies: digital currencies that have no person or institution managing their issuance, have no authority regulating them, and operate throughout a decentralized peer-to-peer network.

While currencies issued by the likes of Amazon and Facebook are arguably more important in the economy, it is cryptocurrencies that drive people's interest in digital currencies. They certainly deserve the attention because of the technical innovation they represent. For example, Bitcoin involves a sophisticated algorithm that solves a long-standing computer-science puzzle, known as the "Byzantine generals problem." In spite of the problem's colorful name, relatively few people have heard about it. And yet most of us have heard about Bitcoin. This is because of the tantalizing implication of a solution to the obscure problem with colorful name—the possibility of payment systems, or even currencies, which operate in a distributed network, with no issuer or institution that controls or manages it and with enough security to withstand malicious attempts to infiltrate it. As we will discuss, this innovation has the potential to meaningfully change the economy, from the way cross-border remittances are sent, to making micropayments economically sustainable, to offering a way of transacting online that protects privacy better than any other method, to changing the way contracts are enforced.

The timing of the innovation could not have been better. Around the same time, the world experienced the largest global financial crisis in modern history. The crisis led some people to question the management of state-issued currencies and the institutions involved in it, in particular, the financial sector and the government. Struggling banks and, indeed, actual bank runs highlighted the potential fragility of traditional financial institutions as safe places for people's deposits, while extraordinary government debt in many countries raised questions about the future value of state-issued currencies. This led some to the conclusion that the time had come for the creation of a money system that is safe, practical for global economic interactions, and importantly, independent of existing large financial institutions and governments. An important aspect of the economic rationale for such a money system has relied on the argument that the current international transfer systems are expensive and inflexible, imposing unreasonable costs on individuals and companies. Beyond these economic rationales, some people, perhaps influenced by a libertarian ideal, also felt the need for a money system that is, simply, out of governments' sight.[1]

Bitcoin has captured media's attention also because of its association with the shadow economy. Some people have always sought secrecy and anonymity in an alternative payment system for the purpose of escaping the law. Since their appearance, the Internet and e-commerce have been used for illegal activities—mostly for the trade of arms and drugs. The size of this illegal trade is hard to estimate but its order of magnitude is in billions of US dollars. One of the most well-known elements of that shadow economy was Silk Road, widely covered in the mainstream media, especially after October 2013, when US law enforcement shut it down and arrested its founder, Ross William Ulbricht. In 2015, Ulbricht was convicted for running the site, and sentenced to life in prison. Silk Road was just one of many—although arguably one of the largest—websites that specialized in matching buyers and sellers of illegal products, operating on the so-called "darknet," a layer of the Internet where activity cannot be (easily) traced back to the physical locations of its participants. For people involved in such illegal

trading activities, a payment system guaranteeing secrecy
and anonymity has always been very attractive proposition.

What fed the media frenzy was the mystique surrounding the first cryptocurrency system, Bitcoin. Bitcoin was
introduced in 2008 by a mysterious character named
Satoshi Nakamoto, whose real identity is unknown. With
a quick and relatively broad adoption, the cryptocurrency
was experiencing a phenomenal success, at least until 2013.
Since then, it has suffered a series of setbacks from a variety of interrelated factors, including a market crash, fraud,
security issues, and regulatory challenges from a number
of governments. More important, Bitcoin's early success
has led to an incredible proliferation of competing cryptocurrencies. Today, the complex ecosystem that emerged
faces considerable uncertainty, raising the question, What
will the future of finance look like after the "Cambrian
Explosion" of cryptocurrencies?

Before even considering this question, one needs to realize that the universe of digital currencies goes far beyond
that of cryptocurrencies. Indeed, a whole new family of
digital currencies has emerged in parallel to Bitcoin and
its competitors. The rise of these currencies is also closely
linked to the emergence of the Internet, and has been
motivated by the needs of large Internet businesses: Amazon, Facebook, Tencent, and so on.

Permanent and ubiquitous connectivity provided by the
Internet has also given rise to these new businesses that
allow a very large number of people to interact in sophisticated ways. Social networks, e-commerce platforms,
online game platforms, or virtual worlds are so-called
"transaction platforms" that create value by facilitating
exchange between their members, who often represent
different groups of consumers: buyers, sellers, advertis-
ers or developers. The nature of the exchange, whether

it is social/commercial, whether it is for entertainment, or whether it concerns a particular professional/business purpose, often defines the business model of the platform, including its value proposition and the way the platform earns its revenue. While these value propositions and revenue models substantially vary across transaction platforms, quite naturally, most of them provide the possibility of economic exchange between their members and between these members and the platform itself. This raises the question of the necessity of a medium of exchange, essentially an efficient payment system, which may be tailored to the special needs of the platform. Many platform businesses have considered introducing a special currency to provide one. Platform-based currencies are, by definition, centralized currencies where the platforms control (to the extent possible) the "rules" governing the use of their currencies.

Interestingly, the core issues guiding the introduction of these platform-based currencies are very different from those of cryptocurrencies. While in the latter case, the goal is to create a fully functional currency to *replace* state-issued currencies, platform-based currencies try to purposefully design their payment systems with specific objectives in mind. This usually boils down to restricting some of the functionalities of their currencies.

Yet, despite these restrictions, platform-based currencies captured the public imagination to the same extent that Bitcoin did, no doubt partly because of these platforms' sheer size and global nature. For example, when Facebook was moving forward with their Facebook Credits in 2011, commentators saw them as a threat to state-issued currencies. "Could a gigantic non-sovereign, like Facebook someday launch a real currency to compete with the dollar, euro, yen and the like?" wrote Matthew Yglesias (2012).

Similarly, renowned payments economist David Evans (2012) wrote: "Social game companies could pay developers around the world in Facebook Credits and small businesspeople could accept Facebook Credits because they could use them to buy other things that they need or reward customers with them. In some countries (especially those with national debts that are greater than their GDPs) Facebook Credits could become a safer currency than the national currency." Similar concerns were expressed when Amazon introduced Amazon Coins in 2013. MarketWatch, affiliated with the *Wall Street Journal*, wrote: "But in the long term what [central banks] should perhaps be most worried about is losing their monopoly on issuing money. A new breed of virtual currencies are starting to emerge—and some of the giants of the web industry such as Amazon.com Inc. are edging into the market."[2] As we will argue below, many of these concerns are exaggerated, even if in some instances, platform-based currencies have had an impact much beyond the business of their issuers.

The goal of this book is to explore the young and dynamic universe of digital currencies to understand their origins and their meaning for our economies. We approach these currencies from the viewpoint of economists, analyzing the needs they fulfill for customers and merchants, the incentives they create for their users, and the way they compete with other potential currencies in the marketplace. Whenever possible, we will do that in a way that abstracts away from technical details of how digital currencies work, making this book suitable for people with little experience or education in computer science, cryptography, and so on. Sometimes we won't be able to avoid talking about technical aspects of a currency—for example, we could scarcely avoid discussing the ingenious algorithm that underlies cryptocurrencies such as Bitcoin—but we will attempt to do so in a way that is as approachable as possible. Rather than create a technical manual, we intend to describe the economic forces governing the evolution of digital currencies.

The objective is to understand why certain models seem to succeed over others: what drives competition between alternative currencies, which currency is likely to prevail if one currency can replace another, and what design features (or restrictions) make sense in given economic or business contexts.

To this end, we will start at the very beginning: we will describe how human societies invented money, how money facilitated transactions, and how weaknesses in the design of money led to innovation and improvements in the way we pay for things. Digital currencies may seem far removed from such history, or even prehistory, of money. However, this historical overview allows us to identify some of the core economic forces that drive the use of different types of money, highlight the specific needs that money serves, and illustrate the key attributes that money should have. These needs and attributes are remarkably universal, and they are as important now as they were centuries ago. Their analysis will lay the groundwork for our subsequent discussion of digital currencies and give us a framework in which to analyze them.

Such a framework is critically important. Without it, it can be difficult to understand what exactly is going on in the digital currency universe. Much of the narrative surrounding digital currencies is a bit sensationalist, undoubtedly influenced by the tumultuous events surrounding the introduction of digital currencies, or the spectacular developments in Bitcoin—not only its rise to immense popularity but also the less optimistic episodes of the Silk Road shutdown or the closing of the Mt. Gox exchange.

Starting with an economic framework will help us see through the confusion to better understand the phenomenon of digital currencies and its potential to change our economy.

In the next part of the book, we will use this framework to explore the universe of platform-based digital currencies that are centrally managed by the businesses that have introduced them. We will analyze the economic forces that made it attractive for Amazon to issue the Amazon Coin or for Facebook to issue Facebook Credits, and why Facebook decided to shut it down soon afterward. Here, we will also discuss what drives the platform's choice of particular design features for its currency.

It turns out that platform-based digital currencies could hardly function as money in the broad sense of the word—not because they are inherently flawed, but because platforms issuing them go to great pains to disable the main functions that are necessary for a widely adopted currency. We will see that this should not be surprising: such restrictions fit well with the platforms' business models and make their currencies more useful in generating a higher profit for the platform.

A widespread adoption, and perhaps even crowding out state-issued currencies, is something often discussed in the context of decentralized digital currencies, or cryptocurrencies such as Bitcoin. We discuss these innovations in the last part of the book. We look at the still ongoing evolution of their design, the value they provide over and above existing alternatives, and some of the challenges they currently face. We again come back to our economic framework and show that many of cryptocurrencies' features are specifically designed to address a particular economic need that has in the past been fulfilled by a corresponding feature of traditional—that is, non-digital—money. This helps us identify features that might be flashy and broadly discussed but that do not change the economics of a cryptocurrency and that make a new cryptocurrency, for all practical purposes, about as useful or as promising as an earlier one. We also look into the ecosystem that cryptocurrencies exist in, focusing on its more economically meaningful parts. For example, we discuss the evolution and the role of online cryptocurrency exchanges and discuss how effectively they function as part of the cryptocurrency infrastructure.

Finally, we discuss the competition between various cryptocurrencies (at the time of writing, there are a few hundred of them that are actively traded) and, perhaps more tantalizingly, the competition between a cryptocurrency and the traditional, state-issued currencies such as the US dollar.

Such discussions often turn into speculation about the future, a temptation we have not managed to resist. At the same time, we clearly recognize that it is too early to paint an exact picture, given the broad scale experimentation still under way. More important, such forecasts are particularly difficult in the light of the uncertainty about how governments will respond to the emergence of digital currencies. In this respect, our book is not a policy piece about central banking or currency regulation. Rather, it is an analysis of the economic forces that drive the emergence and efficient use of competing money systems applied to the digital world.

Chapter 2

Medium of Exchange:
Ever-Present Competition

Digital currencies are only a recent innovation, and their widespread use is still a thing of the future. It is fit, however, to begin our investigation by looking into the past. In fact, we will start not only well before the digital era but also before the development of money itself. We do not intend to provide a comprehensive overview of the history of money here.[1] Rather, in our discussion we will focus on the attributes of different currencies and the various economic needs that money serves. In historical perspective, we can analyze competitive forces that make some media of exchange more successful than others in satisfying those needs. We will later see that digital currencies can be successful only if they satisfy such needs as well as, or better than, the traditional currencies we already have in use.

We will also overview the various objects and technologies that have served as money or, more broadly, as medium of exchange. We will see examples of the coexistence of various currencies, episodes that suggest a tantalizing possibility that, in the future, digital currencies may coexist not only alongside other digital currencies but also side by side with traditional money.

Finally, we will talk about competition between different currencies. Again, insights from this analysis will be useful in later discussion. For example, digital currencies are being introduced alongside traditional money, and necessarily must compete with it. Eventually, if digital currencies win more widespread adoption, we may need to turn these arguments around and use them to discuss whether traditional money can survive long-term in the presence of digital currencies.

With this roadmap in mind, let's move on and start with a brief history of how we trade.

2.1. THE MEDIUM OF EXCHANGE— HISTORICAL OVERVIEW

If you asked your friends why modern economies need money, they would most likely answer "to buy things." This answer would be as simple as it is deceptive. It is certainly true that we need money to facilitate trade, but there was a time in human history when transactions occurred without any money. Most of us have heard about barter, exchange of a product or service directly for another product, without the use of money. But the first economic transactions likely predate even that development. In essence, the earliest transactions were based on trust.

There was no need for money in the preagrarian hunter-gatherer groups.[2] The members of the group were all responsible for a communal provision of goods. The group kept track of each member's contribution and imposed penalties to minimize potential free-riding. The collective memory of the group served as a ledger or perhaps a prehistoric bank account. Members who contributed to the well-being of the group could count on being reciprocated in the future. The side benefit of this simple but ingenious arrangement was credit. A member of a group could potentially count on receiving goods and services even if he or she had not yet earned enough "brownie points" to justify them. As long as the group remembered about the transaction, they could expect the member to repay it with good deeds in the future. If the member didn't, then the group could presumably discipline the member by not allowing him or her to participate in the system going forward.

Of course, counting on collective memory only works if the group is of a relatively small size. Over time, groups grew larger; for example, people started settling in early cities. Eventually, people were unable to keep track of individual contributions. Moreover, as different groups started trading with each other, it became necessary to trade with people who were less familiar, and therefore whose prior contributions were unknown and who could hardly be disciplined for the failure to repay for a product in the future.

Without the help of collective memory and group-imposed discipline, transactions became risky: you could no longer be certain that people you trade with would repay you later. Nonetheless, when people see sufficiently large gains from trade, they usually find a way to realize them. The simplest way to do so is to exchange good immediately, without waiting for an uncertain repayment in the future. So, the unfamiliarity of traders did not stop transactions completely but did force them to be based on an immediate exchange of goods for goods: barter.

Barter works very well—as long as you find a seller offering something you want and if at the same time you have something the seller wants in return. In practice, this "double coincidence of wants" may happen fairly infrequently.[3] This is an important problem that limits trade. If you want to obtain a particular good, it may already be difficult for you to find somebody who has that good to offer; it will be even rarer that you might have something that person wants in return. You may need to rely on longer chains of buyers and sellers—to get something person A wants, I need to trade with person B first. But, of course, it may be even more difficult to find three or more people with suitably aligned holdings and wants and to get them to come to the same place at the same time. Affecting all trades at the same time is also safer. With more parties the first person to hand over their good is the last one to receive the traded good. There is risk that something will go wrong along the way, and the first person in the chain may lose their original good and not receive much in return.

Barter has one more drawback: the timing coincidence. For example, many products are seasonal and may be difficult to store for longer periods of time. In the fall, you may have some berries that you'd be happy to exchange for meat when the winter comes—but since winter is still a few months away, you won't be able to exchange the goods in a pure barter transaction. So, for a barter transaction to be successful, the two sides not only need to want their respective goods but also need to want them and have them available at the same time. Because of such frictions, many potential trades may not occur, leaving the parties that would have benefited from trade worse off.

As societies grew larger, and as new trade opportunities between various groups arose, these frictions and the foregone benefits of trade increased. Emergence of money in such a situation is not inevitable, but the potential benefits may have eventually become so large that they could no longer be ignored. This illustrates the main function of money, intuitively obvious to most people: money is there to facilitate trade, to overcome the double coincidence and timing problems and allow us to obtain the goods and services that we need.

Those early societies that coordinated on using tokens or intermediate goods had more opportunities to trade. The earliest kinds of such intermediate goods, dating back at least to about 3000 BC, was related to foodstuffs such as barley. Using popular foodstuffs helped alleviating the first problem, the coincidence of wants. Everybody in a society consumed similar foodstuffs, making them a product that was attractive to all society members ("we all could use more barley"). Of course, the innovation was that people started accepting barley not only for their own consumption but also in expectation of using the barley for other future transactions. It is likely that this innovation was not decreed by a ruler ("we will all use barley as money") but rather occurred organically. In either case, money, in the sense we typically mean it nowadays, was born. However, this earliest money also served another useful role: it was food.

The foodstuffs used to facilitate trade differed across societies. Barley, likely the first historical example, was used in ancient Mesopotamia. Salt has been used in China in the thirteenth century and in Ethiopia from the sixteenth century until the twentieth century, whereas the Aztec empire adopted cacao beans. All these examples share some important traits. First, they were relatively uniform and easy to divide. One can make smaller or larger units, by weight or volume (barely), by breaking smaller and larger pieces (salt) or collecting smaller or larger amounts (cacao beans). If you measure barley using a standard cup, the cup will hold a similar amount of the foodstuff currency this year and the next, at home or in a neighboring village.

Only relatively durable foodstuffs were adopted as money. In this, they clearly dominated other articles of food such as perishable fruit, fish, or milk. Nonetheless, they could not be stored indefinitely, and sometimes they lasted only for one season or at most a few seasons. Foodstuffs deteriorate quickly for a range of reasons. The foodstuff money could perish when exposed to the elements or, more prosaically, could be eaten by animals.

The money kept evolving and, around 1200 BC, an innovation appeared: money based on tokens that were not related to food. Perhaps the most well known of such tokens were cowry shells, in widespread use in Africa for hundreds of years. The range of such money was, however, much greater. To give just two more colorful examples, until the nineteenth century whale teeth served as money on Fiji and, in the Admiralty Islands, dog teeth played the same role until the twentieth century.[4]

This token-based money had clear advantages relative to foodstuffs. The tokens would keep for much longer than one season. They were also easier to store or transport over longer distances. An important feature of token-based currencies was that the tokens represented value in a more abstract, symbolic way than barley or cacao did, as they had less intrinsic value than food did. Usually they had cultural meaning, and they were also used for decoration. Interestingly, it is not clear whether they developed into currency *because* they had cultural meaning or whether they gained the meaning because they could be used in exchanges and therefore represented more value.

Along these advantages, there were a few distinct drawbacks. While foodstuffs that were used as currencies were relatively uniform, the tokens used as money varied greatly in shapes, sizes, and colors. These differences, naturally occurring in shells, teeth, and so on, made it more difficult for people using the currency to agree on which "prices" they represented. For example, a fish might be worth three dog teeth, but perhaps the seller would demand four teeth instead if the teeth were particularly small. In some cases, such differences between tokens were used to the advantage. For example, on the Yap Island, blue-lipped cowrie shells, a rarer type than the more popular yellow-lipped kind, served as a "higher denomination" currency.

A particular type of token money were metal pieces. The first use of metal as currency that we know about occurred in ancient Mesopotamia, in 2500 BC.[5] Metal proved to be even more durable than shells or teeth. It was also easily divisible into smaller units, and these units could be directly compared with each other based on their weight. This represented an improvement over naturally occurring shells or teeth.

Nonetheless, metals had not completely solved the problem of non-uniform units. While it was easy to weigh pieces of metal, there were several types of metals in common usage: copper, silver, and, of course, gold. Moreover, even one type of a metal may have differed in purity. These differences led to difficulties and additional risks in conducting transactions, particularly when metal money was used by people without specialized knowledge about it. Risk around the value of received payment would make some sellers wary, and they may avoid some trades that could otherwise be beneficial.

The problem of non-uniform units was the likely driver of the next innovation: metal-based coins. These uniform pieces of metal, with a stamp indirectly certifying weight and purity, represented uniform units. Two coins with the same stamp were considered equivalent; different stamps were readily recognized as agreed-on indicators of the weight of the coin or type of metal. This made transactions—exchanges of metal for goods—much easier. One did not need to have scales handy and know how to use them or have expertise to judge metal purity. One could rely on the stamp as the indicator of value.[6] This, of course, worked well when people trusted the stamp. Typically, mints would be directly or indirectly controlled by the sovereign. The benefit of the coin then depended on people's trust in the authority and integrity of the ruler. When people did not trust the stamp, they reverted to older methods of weighing and checking the purity of the metal.

The first coins were introduced in the kingdom of Lydia in the seventh century BC. They were minted from electrum, a naturally occurring mixture of gold and silver, but the silver and gold coins soon followed. An interesting innovation at that time was that Lydian coins were relatively small, making it easier to store and transport the currency. While earlier metal was used for large value transactions, each coin was worth a few days of laborer's work or a small part of a harvest. This opened up what could be called a retail market to more trading opportunities.

The Lydian invention turned out to be more attractive than the earlier types of money were. The invention quickly spread throughout the Mediterranean, and metal coins of different values and sizes became the main tool of the trade in the Western world until the Renaissance. The basic model remained unchanged until now. Coins are still metal discs with a stamp certifying the value of the piece.

The next significant innovation in money was paper money. Historically, it was first introduced in China in the eighth century. It is possible that the idea of paper money was brought to Europe by Marco Polo. In Europe, paper money became popular during the Renaissance, when Italian bankers introduced bills of credit. Both in China and in Europe, paper was substituted for metal because paper was cheaper, easier, and safer to transport. A person carrying paper money was less conspicuous than was a carriage with valuable metal. Therefore, carriers of paper money were less likely to be attacked on the roads. Both because of lower risk of attack and because only the person carrying the paper needed guarding and not the carriage with metal pieces, one needed to hire fewer guards to travel safely than when transporting the same value of metal.

For several centuries paper money represented a claim on metal money. It was done through different types of promissory notes. Receipts for deposits are the simplest one. When a person deposited gold with a Renaissance goldsmith-banker, he (usually a he at that time) would get a receipt. With this receipt the gold could be withdrawn from the goldsmith. Originally the receipts were personal, but later they became payable to the bearer. That allowed for transferability, and thus the receipts could be used in transactions in lieu of the gold itself.

Later, when banks were issuing banknotes, holding a dollar note from the Bank of Augusta, Georgia, meant that the Bank of Augusta would at any time redeem that note for specie; that is, gold or silver coins. It was true, in principle, until the gold standard was abandoned in 1970s.[7]

After the gold standard was dropped, paper money was no longer a claim on metal or any other good. It became fiat money, money "on the say-so." Countries made them legal tender, in the sense that they were accepted as payment of taxes and debts. Merchants needed to accept it, unless they explicitly stated that they would not. But most importantly, paper money is accepted because the sellers know they can spend it as money. It has no intrinsic value, unless you count the recycling value of the paper. Their value is purely symbolic.

It is true not only about the paper money. Even though metal may have more intrinsic value than paper does, modern coins' value derives from the number stamped on them. The coins are no longer minted of gold and silver but are minted of less-valued metals such as copper and nickel. The symbolic value of most coins is larger than the value of metal in them. But in some cases, it costs more to make them than their face value. For this reason the Canadian Mint stopped issuing one cent coins in 2013.

While today we accept paper money as one of the most common forms of currency, it was not the case historically. There were often problems in introducing paper money, for example, because the populace did not consider it as trustworthy as metal coins and possibly feared overissuance. In some regions, notably China, paper money representing metal money was introduced successfully because it was imposed and guaranteed by the state. The state in fact resorted to executing people who refused to comply, and to confiscating other potential means of payment, like metal and gems.[8] In Europe, paper money had more difficulties in becoming generally adopted. European states did not impose as strong of an enforcement, and neither did they guarantee the paper money's value. There were several cases of governments overissuing paper money that later was not redeemed at the promised value.[9] This created mistrust of paper money and hindered its widespread adoption.

The final development, which brings us to the current times, is electronic money.[10] Most often when people think of electronic money, they think of credit cards. Credit cards did not start as electronic. They did not even start as plastic. They started as cardboard cards back in the 1950s. Credit card systems are based on a ledger. Transactions are recorded and reported to an institution holding the ledger and the accounts. The institution, usually a bank, checks whether the funds about to be spent are available, bundles transactions for billing the account holder, and usually also offers credit services. The credit card gives information about the account and the system where the account is held.

Introduction of digital technologies allowed for electronic reporting of the transactions, sped up authorization and decreased fraud. But ultimately, it is a digital way of moving money that has a physical counterpart. A different type of digital money—the focus of the following chapters—is money that only exists digitally. Free from the physical counterpart, it may have different properties than money we know from the history.

The widespread adoption of the more modern forms of money—metal coins, paper money, and increasingly, electronic money—is driven by their advantages over earlier forms. But even nowadays, there are still situations when the earlier types of money reappear. For example, the shortage of the usual currency in prisoner of war camps led to the use of cigarettes as token currency. The same token has been adopted as currency in the informal economies in prisons. Interestingly, when smoking was banned in some prisons, cigarettes disappeared, but money did not: prisoners started using cans of mackerel as currency.[11] Table 2.1 summarizes the various types of money we discussed and gives a short overview of the advantages and drawbacks of each stage.

2.2. WHAT ROLES DOES MONEY SERVE?

The key role of money is to facilitate trade. Voluntary trade means that each party prefers to receive the goods that the other party has rather than retain the goods that they were originally holding. Therefore, such a trade improves

Table 2.1 A brief overview of the major innovations in the history of money

Money	Time	Positive attributes	Negative attributes
Food based (salt, barley, cacao)	3000 BC	Easily divisible units (e.g., by weight)	Difficult to transport, perishable (eaten by animals)
Tokens (cowry shells, dog teeth, whale teeth)	1200 BC	Longer lasting, easier to store	Non-uniform units (naturally occurring in different shapes, sizes, and color)
Metal	2500 BC	Long lasting, easier to store, easily divisible units (e.g., by weight)	Non-uniform due to varying purity; heavy
Metal coins	Seventh century BC	Uniform units (two coins equal), long lasting	Heavy
Paper money	Eighth century AD	Uniform units, mimicked divisibility of units (different denomination), easier to carry	Easy to counterfeit
Electronic money	Twentieth century AD	Uniform units, divisibility of units, even easier to carry	Easy to copy

the well-being of the parties trading. However, as we saw in our historical overview, there are important frictions that limit trade or make it more difficult. Money is an important innovation in that it alleviates some of those frictions.

The adoption of a given type of money will depend on how well the money's attributes satisfy consumers' economic needs. We discussed a number of such attributes— for example, divisibility, ease of storage and transport—in our overview and we present them in its summary table. We now discuss them more systematically.

Economists often use the following three-part definition of money: (1) unit of account, (2) medium of exchange, and (3) store of value. This definition means that two people can agree how much a good is worth in terms of money (that's part 1); people accept the money when they are selling the good, because they believe it will be accepted elsewhere when they want to exchange it for a good they want to buy (part 2); and money will not lose its value drastically between the time people get it and the time they spend it to buy something else (part 3).

These three characteristics make it possible for money to facilitate trade. Each of these dimensions is important. If we know that even one is missing, we would probably not accept a given kind of money in a transaction.

There are, however, some issues with this definition. First of all, it is somewhat circular. In essence, it says that money is something that is being used as money. In this sense, it just describes an equilibrium. What it cannot do is tell us whether a can of mackerel or a Zimbabwean dollar is money. Moreover, the definition sounds like three yes-or-no questions, suggesting that if you answer "yes" three times, what you are evaluating is money. That's not the case.

For example, there is nothing that could serve as medium of exchange in *all* transactions and nothing that could potentially store value *forever*.[12] If we take this interpretation, suddenly perfectly good currencies do not satisfy the definition. Take the euro or the Swedish krona or the Polish zloty. Are they good store of value for the next 300 years? That is doubtful. Similarly, the Confederate dollar was money when it was used, but turned out not to be a good store of value—it became worthless after the Civil War. The currency needs to store the value for long enough that the person who gets the currency can reasonably believe that he or she can spend it (a few days, weeks, months . . . the definition is purposely a bit vague on the details here). Otherwise it just would not be a good medium of exchange.

Moreover, this definition is meant to apply for a particular environment, for instance, a geographic area. Consider for example the Swedish krona. Few people would deny that the krona is money. It certainly satisfies the textbook definition, serving as a unit of account, a store of value, and medium of exchange—with one qualification. You can easily transact in Swedish kronas in Sweden, but they may not be generally accepted elsewhere. You are very unlikely to be able to use them in a corner store in the United States.

We see that the textbook definition has an important drawback—it does not state the boundaries, does not define the environment for which it should apply. We cannot apply it universally, as that would make it completely vacuous. For example, even the US dollar, the most global of currencies we have, is not accepted *everywhere*. Abroad, one might be able to exchange it for the local currency, but not all local stores and institutions would accept US dollars directly as a means of payment.

Thus, there is a whole spectrum of how broadly or narrowly this definition applies. In fact, we would argue that some innovations deserve to be called money even though their scope is limited to a few particular transaction types. As we will see, many digital currencies operate with such restrictions, being limited to a particular type of (digital) environment and to only some specific goods that you can transact or use within that environment, for example, a sword for your avatar in the multiplayer online game World of Warcraft. Purists might argue that this disqualifies such digital currencies as "money"—after all, they are not a *generally* accepted medium of exchange for all, or even most, transactions. But then how does it differ from the Swedish krona?

Money should facilitate trade. It may facilitate trade in some geographic area or facilitate only a specific kind of trade. The more limited the trade it can facilitate, the more limited the currency. At some point one can say it is so limited it is no longer a currency. Unfortunately, deciding where that point lies could easily become just an issue of semantics, particularly in an area so new, dynamic, and full of borderline cases as digital currencies.

Given the limits to the textbook definition of money— limiting a currency to geographic region or transaction type—it is easy to see how a few different types of money could coexist at the same time, something that has occurred multiple times in the past, as we will discuss in the next section.

What Makes Good Money?
Importantly, these limitations do not detract from the incredible usefulness of the definition. Working with this definition, and analyzing the traits that money needs to exhibit, has allowed economists to explain why some goods are more fit to be used as money than others are. For example, barley is a good unit of account, because it is divisible. But it is not durable, and it could lose value between one transaction and another; thus it is not a very good store of value. Houses are inconvenient money for

different reasons. Even though they are very durable, they are hardly divisible and are often incomparable, making them a poor unit of account. It is also cumbersome to exchange ownership of a house—at least, harder than to hand over pieces of metal. So real estate is also a poor medium of exchange. This is why handy goods that are small enough to carry around and to pass to another person serve the function better.

We can see how the different attributes of different types of money relate to how well each of the three functions is fulfilled. Whether the units are uniform or non-uniform affects the unit of account function. The same uncertainty of whether a fish is worth three or four dog teeth, depending on the quality of teeth, makes it hard to assess and compare the value of different goods systematically. This uncertainty may increase the need for bargaining, and it makes transactions more time consuming. Thus, such goods do not facilitate trade as well as otherwise similar goods that are uniform across units. On this dimension, barley may be better than dog teeth are. And since barley from different fields may have slightly different qualities, the coins and banknotes that we use today are better than barley.

Similarly, other attributes influence how well a potential currency does as a store of value. Goods that are long lasting and easy to store safely do better as currencies. To take an extreme example, a radioactive element with a short half-life would make for a very poor currency (although, admittedly, its failure as a store of value may not be the biggest problem with it).[13]

Other attributes influence the role of a good as a medium of exchange. Clearly, a well-performing medium of exchange should be easily divisible. Some trades may not be possible if there are no sufficient denominations.

Goods that are light and easy to carry do well as medium of exchange: carrying around heavy and unwieldy pieces of metal is inconvenient, which makes it tempting to leave such money at home, which in turn may make you miss many opportunities to transact.[14] A good medium of exchange is also not too susceptible to fraud—that is, it is difficult to falsify or duplicate. Scarcity matters for both a medium of exchange and a store of value. If there is abundance of a particular good, and it is easy to get it in unlimited quantities, this good would not make good money. Consider, for example the case of sand on a beach. Why would a seller give up a good for sand if he could easily get the sand and keep the good? To be scarce, money needs to be costly to produce—mine, collect, or grow. For example, metals that function well as money—gold and silver—are costly to mine. It was not so much the case with foodstuff money, like barley. Nonetheless, it could still function as money because it did not last long. It was consumed or perished otherwise, and the supply of foodstuff money needed to be replenished every year just to keep the same level. For metal, which is durable and lasts for centuries, to be scarce enough to be money it needs to be more costly to produce, so that only a small amount is added every year. If as much gold were added every year as barley, gold would quickly lose its value.

Durability of metal also provided a more stable money supply. Barley harvest may be more or less abundant every year. And as supply of money fluctuates, so will the prices. In a year of a good harvest, there is a lot of barley everywhere and the prices of non-barley goods increase. Unstable (that is, changing and unmanaged) supply leads to a greater variability in prices. Such variability intensifies uncertainty, which in turn may create frictions in trade. It makes metal, with its more stable supply, more preferred as money. Of course, even metal money supply may experience large fluctuations. The primary example is the discovery of the Americas, which brought large amounts of gold and silver to the European economy.

For most of the history of money, people could choose whether to "produce" money or produce goods and services that could be exchanged for money. Growing barley, mining metal, or looking for cowry shells is how one would produce money directly. But for that, one would need to make a choice to grow more barley instead of grazing cows, or abandon their farm to look for gold in California's rivers. Such choice was no longer possible with the introduction of paper money. Paper money was cheap to produce, and its scarcity came from state regulation in the form of strong constraints on who could produce money and how much. Thus, scarcity of paper money was imposed artificially, while scarcity of earlier money resulted from the cost of their production. As we will see later, the issue of scarcity is very important for digital currency schemes, as digital money could sometimes be made "with a click of a mouse." This issue was especially challenging for decentralized digital money systems.

Table 2.2 highlights how various attributes support the three roles of money. In our historical overview, we saw that these roles and attributes influenced the evolution

Table 2.2 Attributes supporting the critical roles of money

Role of money	Attributes supporting the role
Unit of account	Uniform units
Store of value	Long lasting, easy to store securely, scarce
Medium of exchange	Easily divisible, uniform units, light and easy to carry, trustworthy (less susceptible to fraud), scarce

of money and led to gradual improvements in how we transact.

Transaction Costs
The importance of the three roles of money, and the attributes that support them, is related to transaction costs. Broadly speaking, money facilitates trade by lowering transaction costs. And more transaction costs can be overcome when money satisfies its three roles well.

All transactions have some element of costs inherent in them. The costs may come from many drivers. Perhaps the most obvious one is the time needed to conduct a transaction. We saw the importance of this cost already in the earliest human communities, as it was one of the most important costs of barter: you may need to spend a long time to find somebody willing to trade something you have for something you want. To a lesser degree, time costs made unminted pieces of metal inferior to later types of money: you needed to spend time weighing a piece of metal or dividing it into smaller pieces. Another type of cost is related to the effort in changing the ownership of the medium of exchange. For example, money that is particularly heavy or difficult to transport would be costly to deliver to the seller.

Other important costs are the mental costs, for example, having to conduct relatively more complicated arithmetic to complete a transaction that uses many different units of a currency or several different currencies. A related cost is the probability of making a mistake, for example, in deciding how much change to give back, or in distinguishing differing qualities in dog teeth or pieces of metal that might influence their value.

Besides these costs, there exist transaction costs that are more indirect. After a completed transaction, the seller may need to secure the money he has just obtained, which, depending on the type of money, may be costly. The obvious example here is the protection from theft, for example, hiring guards when transferring money, building safes for storing metal, and so on. Less obvious examples, more relevant for commodities-based currencies, are the need for protection from the elements and vermin, or the need to build large warehouses to store your money; both are quite important when the money is, for example, barley.

Finally, lost opportunities—foregone transactions that did not occur—are another type of transaction cost. Money that does not satisfy its three roles well may not be able to facilitate as many transactions, and each transaction that does not happen is a loss to the potential buyer and seller and to the overall economy. The attributes of the good serving as money may contribute to the loss of transactions, for example heaviness or use of unknown metal. Because of these attributes, potential trading partners may view the transaction as too costly to conduct, or perhaps too risky, and decide not to go ahead with it. Transactions may be lost also when units of the currency are not sufficiently divisible. For example, if a particular fish is worth 4.25 dog teeth to the seller and 4.75 teeth to the buyer, their trade would be beneficial for both sides, but it will not occur because dog teeth are not divisible. A transaction might be conducted for 4 teeth or perhaps for 5 teeth— but it won't, as either option would make one of the parties strictly worse off than not transacting at all would.

The transaction costs argument helps us understand why gold has been a long time winner in the money arena. Gold is durable and divisible, and it can be weighted for a uniform unit of account. Moreover, gold has been culturally valuable, because it does not change its appearance over time.

Trust and Counterfeiting

Gold helps us highlight a particular attribute of money that will become important with digital currencies: trust. Money should be a good store of value, and scarcity is often thought to guarantee the value over time. It is also relatively more difficult to falsify—or, at least, tools such as the touchstone were developed to check the purity of gold.

Trusting that a currency is genuine is an important prerequisite for conducting a transaction. Although nowadays we usually think about counterfeiting in the context of paper money, this nefarious procedure is much older than that. For example, metal coins were often "clipped," making them of lower weight than they should be according to their stamp. To prevent debasement, coin edges were stamped or rimmed, making it easier for users to identify whether pieces of metal were cut from a coin, changing its weight and its value. Nowadays coins' value no longer comes from their weight. Nonetheless, many contemporary coins have rimmed edges, due to this legacy. In another type of counterfeiting, metal coins or unminted metal pieces could contain a lesser-valued metal inside, obscured by the correct metal outside. Imagine, for example, a copper core covered in a silver coating to imitate a silver coin. Human ingenuity is limitless. Even commodity-based money was falsified. Consider cacao, used in the Aztec empire as money. Counterfeiters falsified that currency by filling an empty cacao husk with mud and sealing it.[15]

Counterfeiting considerations are particularly important in the context of digital currencies. Digital technology makes it very easy and cheap to make perfect copies of digitally stored information: files, code, passwords, addresses, and so on. In the music industry, it resulted in large-scale piracy, which changed how this industry operates. In the context of money, it gives rise to the so-called double-spending issue.

In the next chapters, we will analyze the various roles of money in the context of digital currencies. We will then see that many of the attributes are as important to traditional (physical) and to digital currencies. We will see that digital money may have significant advantages when it comes to facilitating trade, making it cheaper and faster. We will also see that fraud, and hence the lack of trust, has been a particular challenge for attempts to create money in the digital world.

2.3. COMPETING MONEY

Most of us are used to one particular type of money (say, US dollars), and we think of that "the money" as just being there. There is nothing wrong with this perception; in most places, at a given time and place, just one particular currency is in use. But as with any other product, money competes with other money. If we look closely, we will see this competition all the time. In the historical context, silver competed with barley, metal coins competed with unminted metal, and paper money competed with gold. Interestingly, multiple competing currencies often coexisted, if only for some time. Venetian ducats and Florence's florins competed with other coins throughout medieval Europe, and now the euro and the US dollar compete in international transactions. In fact, without competition there would be no change—a new currency or a new form of money is introduced into an economy that typically already has an incumbent currency. The new innovation can only survive, and perhaps eventually win widespread adoption, if it can successfully compete with the incumbents. But then, what determines the outcome of such competition?

2.3.1. Coexistence Is Costly

There are clear costs to having multiple currencies within an economy. We can divide these costs into two broad categories: cognitive costs and costs of exchange.

The cognitive costs arise from the mental hardship of having to compare prices and values quoted in various currencies. One needs to not only compare different units when deciding whether to buy something but possibly also perform some mental arithmetic when selecting the banknotes and coins to pay for the purchase or when accepting change from the purchase. Consider for example the coinage system in England. That system historically included farthings, pennies, shillings, crowns, pounds, and guineas, some made of different metals, and thus changing value to one another. Finally, the relative value of these different units was fixed in 1717. For example, the value of a guinea had fluctuated between 20 and 30 shillings, before being fixed at 21 shillings in 1717. A pound contained 20 shillings, so a guinea was worth 1 pound and 1 shilling. A shilling contained 12 pennies, and each pence contained 4 farthings (and, in earlier times, it varied between 8 and 4 farthings to a penny). A crown was a quarter of a pound.

Other European countries also used multiple units. For example, prerevolutionary France had a system of currency that rivaled the English one in terms of its complexity. The central unit of the system was the louis d'or, which consisted of 10 livres. Each livre consisted of 20 sols. Each sol consisted of 12 deniers. And those were just gold coins. Among silver ones, 60 sous constituted 1 silver ecu. The relative value of gold and silver coins was changing with time. Such multiplicity created frictions. The local population must have been used to this mélange. Nonetheless, one suspects that this multiplicity of types of coinage created much scope for mistakes and confusion. And with similarly complicated and incompatible systems in other countries, it made international trade more confusing. Eventually, such frictions were resolved by adopting the metric system. The adoption of the metric system for coinage started with the United States and France in the late eighteenth century. The United Kingdom had been a holdout in its long-standing refusal to adopt the metric system in their currency. The system with pound as a unit and 100 (new) pennies to a pound—dropping other units, like guinea and farthings—was only introduced in 1971. The change of the metric system can also be seen in the light of the mental cost of handling money: if one operates in decimal system, it is much easier to add, subtract or multiply values expressed in currencies quoted in the base of 100 (as opposed to, say, 21, the number of shillings in a guinea).

Technology can help diminish these costs, although arguably not eliminate them. For example, cellphones and widespread Internet coverage make it easy to convert prices quoted in a foreign currency into your home currency. Still, there is, and likely always will be, some inconvenience in, say, having to turn to your cellphone every time you want to buy something. Moreover, even if referring to your cellphone is hassle-free, it does not preclude the second large category of costs: costs of exchange.

In economies that use multiple different currencies, people bear the cost of having to exchange one currency for another. This cost cannot be avoided at the level of the overall economy: even if you decide to only ever accept and spend one type of currency, some of the parties you transact with will need to exchange your favored currency for the currency of choice of their other customers or suppliers.

To better illustrate the costs of multiple different currencies circulating in an economy, let's consider the state banking era of the United States in the period between 1786 and 1963. In those early days of the country, the US government minted coins but did not issue paper money. The reason for this setup was that government-printed money was subject to controversy after the overissuance of Continentals during the War of Independence.

Even though the US government refrained from issuing paper currency, private banks printed their own paper money, eventually supplying the market with a plethora of various banknotes. The issuing private banks were established based on individual states' legislation, and virtually every private bank issued its own notes. The scale of this phenomenon reflects the fact that in 1860 there were over 1,500 banks in the United States, out of which 54 were in just New York City.

The banks were not allowed to simply print money at will. By the requirement of the legislature, the notes they issued had to be backed by assets, and the issuing bank had the obligation to redeem the notes for specie, that is, metal coins. A failure to exchange the notes brought for redemption into specie was a serious offense, and it could be a cause for the bank's failure. On average, 0.5 percent of banks failed annually, although there were years when even 5 percent of banks failed.

With thousands of different types of banknotes circulating in the economy, not all notes were treated equally. For example, it quickly became clear that a five dollar note from one bank could be worth less than a five dollar note from another bank. These discounts made the exchange of banknotes and trade more costly.

The reason for different valuation of notes often related to the difficulty and risk of successful redemption of the note for specie. To redeem the note one had to go to the bank that issued it. This may have been easy for your local bank, but would have been difficult and perhaps too expensive if you had a note issued by a bank far away. If you still undertook the journey, and if you were particularly unlucky, you might have found that the bank you were going to had failed by the time you got there. Indeed, researchers found that the discounts varied geographically, and discounts were generally lower for banks that were local and, hence, more known to people living in a given area.[16]

The discount also captured the risk of a bank failing. If such a risk was high, it was less certain that the banknote could be redeemed. Failing banks either would not redeem notes at all or would redeem them at a fraction of the face value. Thus, accepting notes from some banks was considered riskier than accepting other banks' notes was. It may have come from general knowledge that a particular bank was in trouble, but also from lack of familiarity with the bank. Somebody who lived in Philadelphia may have had less information about Boston banks and may have been less willing to accept banknotes issued by those banks. This was another reason why the notes from far away banks traded at a larger discount.

Uncertainty about the value of a banknote ties to another phenomenon: forgery. Counterfeiting was rampant. With the multitude of note designs, it was difficult to keep track of what a genuine note of a particular bank should look like. Again, it was more likely that banknotes from afar were counterfeits, as people were less familiar with their design. More colorfully, forgers would sometimes make up entire banks and banknotes issued by these (fictional) banks. In an environment with hundreds of different issuers, forgers sometimes managed to get away with this ploy, but ultimately it contributed to people's general aversion to less popular banknotes or banknotes from geographically distant locales.

You can imagine that most people were simply unable to keep track of all these issues and nuances. Not surprisingly, brokers appeared who were willing to accept various banknotes and exchange them for one another—for a price. The brokers in many cities would publish weekly, biweekly, or monthly "counterfeit detectors" or "banknote reporters"—publications listing known counterfeits and often quoting discounts for trading genuine notes of different banks. In those publications merchants would find advice such as "better refuse all 5s" from Webster Bank of Boston, Massachusetts, or "beware of all denominations of the old fraudulent bank of this name" for New York Exchange Bank.[17] These reporters were available to the public —again, for a price. But even if you had one, consulting it was time consuming for merchants and others who were using them.

Overall, the costs of having this multitude of banknotes were high. They included both cognitive and economic costs. The latter included the direct costs of conducting transactions (e.g., having to buy a currency reporter), and the costs of bearing the extra risk and uncertainty when dealing with various banknotes. All this created frictions in trade and a burden to the overall economy.[18]

The desire to avoid these costs is an important driver of competition among currencies and may eventually push the economy to one generally adopted currency. As it turns out, there is also another powerful incentive operating in the same direction: network effects.

2.3.2. Network Effects

Competition between currencies is different from competition between most goods, and one aspect plays a key role here: money exhibits what in economics is termed "network effects." Simply put, an object is more useful as money if other people are using it as money as well.

Network effects were first recognized in economics literature in the 1980s.[19] To use the most classical example, consider the telephone network. There is no use in owning a telephone if you own the only one. The value a telephone increases as more people buy phones, that is, there are more phones in the network.

Over the past few decades, studying network effects became a vibrant subfield of economics. Tools that economists developed to study networks have been used to analyze, explain, and understand a variety of modern technologies: videogame consoles, computers, or smartphones. The applications are particularly relevant in the context of communication technologies. In fact, it has been observed that what has been named "network effects" does not need a physical network. There is no need for wires like those in the telephone network for network effects to occur.

It turns out that the network effects argument readily applies to money. Suppose you want to introduce a new form of money. Initially, you are the only one who recognizes and accepts that money, making it very difficult to persuade someone else to adopt it as well. After all, if he does, he will initially have only you to trade with. Things are easier if there is already a larger part of the society, hopefully including both potential buyers and sellers, who stand ready to use the currency.

With network effects, we often see a "winner-take-all" dynamics. If two networks are similar but one is larger, the larger one will be more attractive to the new users. Users from the smaller network may also prefer to switch to the larger network. The larger will grow even larger, while the smaller may even disappear. Thus, the winner takes the whole market. Often such a market is efficient, as all users may take advantage of maximal network effect. Because of that, economic research often finds that it is socially optimal when we all use the same technology that generates network effects.

We frequently see such winner-take-all dynamics in the context of money. As with other technologies that generate network effects, money accepted by a larger number of people is more useful than is money used by a few. And since a currency is more useful when more people adopt it, the benefit is maximized when everybody uses the same currency.

In our earlier historical overview, we discussed the appearance of coins in Lydia in the seventh century BC. There were good reasons why coins were a superior technology to unminted metal—for example, the coins with the same mark were uniform, they were all worth the same, and everyone knew what they were worth. They saved time spent on weighing and decreased the probability of cheating. Thus, when two trading parties could use coins or unminted metal, both preferred to use coins. Moreover, the seller knew that he would have an easier time using coins rather than unminted metal in future transactions, so he was more willing to accept them. And as more people used coins, fewer people wanted to use unminted metal. That is, as coins became more popular, their appeal grew and it further increased their popularity. With time coins took over the market for most transactions. Unminted metal was used when coins were not available or when the value of a transaction was very large and one slab of metal was handier than many coins were.

The Renaissance gives us another example of the winner-take-all dynamics in money. During the Renaissance, Italian banking—especially Florentine and Venetian—spread throughout Europe, making the currencies of Florence (florin) and of Venice (ducat) the currencies of choice even in places far away from Italy. With credit from Italian banking houses, many trades were conducted in those currencies, and people became more and more familiar with them. When merchants had a chance to conduct trade in florins and ducats or in some other coins, they preferred florins and ducats. Thus, florins and ducats were becoming more popular, becoming the dominant currencies of Europe, and pushing out other currencies.

Our final example is that of the Maria Theresa thaler. The thaler (a name from which the word "dollar" is derived) was introduced in 1773 in honor of the Austrian empress, the wife of Holy Roman Emperor Francis I. It rapidly became very popular, especially in North Africa and in the Middle East.[20] People became reluctant to use any other currency. The reason why they preferred Maria Theresa thalers is precisely the network effects: they preferred the thalers because they knew that everyone else would also prefer to trade using Maria Theresa thalers, and may not be as inclined to trade using other potential coins. This dynamics reinforced the popularity of Maria Theresa thalers in the region, pushing other coins out.

Maria Theresa died in 1780, but the coin continued to be minted. It was an unusual practice to mint coins with an image of a deceased ruler, so all the coins minted after Maria Theresa's death bore the date 1780. They kept being minted after Napoleon abolished the Holy Roman Empire in 1805 and after the Austro-Hungarian Empire disintegrated after World War I. Later, the Austrian Republic continued to mint them until the Anschluss by Hitler in 1937. Italy minted Maria Theresa thalers in the late 1930s for the use in the conquered territory of Abyssinia (today's Ethiopia). Tellingly, Mussolini's government decided to supply the thalers because the local population in Abyssinia refused to accept substitutes. They were used to and trusted Maria Theresa thalers. The power of the "winner-take-all" effect was such that it was difficult for modern currencies to be successfully introduced into that economy. The effect was not limited to Abyssinia: the thaler was minted in mints from Bombay and Brussels to Utrecht and Vienna. Even after the Second World War, Austria resumed minting the coins in 1956, with the last being minted in 1975. The total number of silver Maria Theresa thalers minted between 1780 and 1975 is estimated at about 400 million. Each one is dated 1780.

With the network effects pushing the economy toward a single currency, why do we observe prolonged episodes in which multiple currencies are in use, for example, the multitude of banknotes during the state banking era in the United States, described earlier? In the case of the banking era, the reason was the external limit imposed by regulation. The coins that won the market, whether florins, ducats, or Maria Theresa thalers, were minted up to the point when the supply of the coins matched the demand. In contrast, banks under state banking laws were kept small (e.g., they could not merge with each other) and they were limited in the value of banknotes they could issue. The issuance was limited by the banks' capital, which in turn was limited by the law. For some small or sparsely populated areas, one bank's supply of banknotes was enough to match the demand. But for most urban areas, the demand for banknotes was much larger than what any one bank could legally provide. This restriction, and the situation it gave rise to, was detrimental for the economy as a whole and some standardization was needed. As we will see below, it was a central authority (essentially, new regulation) that solved the problem: The US government forced all banks and citizens to use the US dollar.

2.3.3. The Difficulty of Introducing a New Currency: Excess Inertia

Time and again we see an innovation—say, a new and promising technology—that has problems penetrating the market and wining market share from the incumbent that may be offering a less efficient technology. Network economics allows us to better understand this tug of war between popularity and ease of use. This interplay, as identified in the economic literature, is one of the characteristic features that we should expect in environments with network effects. Such environments are often too slow in adapting new technology, and they sometimes may fail to adopt it altogether even though it would have been beneficial to do so. Economists call this "excess inertia."[21]

In our historical overview, we saw innovations that were seamlessly introduced into the economy and that eventually won widespread popularity. For example, coins were quickly adopted, and they eventually crowded out the prior incumbent, unminted metal pieces. However, other innovations faced major frictions, slowing down adoption or making it outright impossible.

Such adoption friction was present in the case of paper money. Paper money provides a better technology, in terms of convenience, than metal money does. For example, it is easier to transport. Yet, it took a long time for the Western world to embrace it. In contrast, China adopted paper money much earlier because of the direct enforcement of this innovation by the state.

Similarly, credit cards are more convenient to use than cash is, especially for large-value transactions. They are appealing to customers because they are lighter and safer than cash is, and they eliminate the need to worry about change. Their appeal is somewhat more limited for merchants, who need to pay additional fees to be able to accept credit cards. Nonetheless, for large-value transactions the benefit of increased security may outweigh the cost, because for example the merchant may avoid carrying large amount of cash to the bank. Also, by accepting credit cards, the merchants avoid the risk that the trade would not happen because the customer does not have enough cash on him or her.

And indeed credit cards became very popular, at least by the turn of the century. However, the initial adoption was not very brisk. Despite the advantages of the technology, it was more of a push of the credit card companies than a pull of the customers. There was a lot of mistrust, both on the side of customers and on the side of merchants. To counter that inertia, credit card companies put a lot of effort into educating people and encouraging the use of the system. For example, they give awards for using credit cards, and they advertise their fraud protection plans.

Credit card companies do not issue cards and manage payments only for the social good and the benefits of the market. They are concerned with their own profit. But one could easily imagine that without the active role of credit card companies the market would stick for longer to the traditional but less efficient use of a large amount of cash. Alternatively, the new technology could have fizzled out because each side would worry that the new payment system would not gain enough traction with the other side. Nowadays we can point to the great convenience of using credit cards online and think that the benefit of adoption is clear. But credit cards would probably not be used online if they had not been adopted earlier for brick-and-mortar transactions.

From the examples above, we see that sometimes the ease of use is the prevailing force and the new technology is smoothly adopted, like coins. Sometimes it is adopted with resistance and frictions due to excess inertia, as with paper money and credit cards. And it is possible that sometimes it is not adopted at all. We simply do not observe a failed potential entrant. For instance, it may be that the popularity of the Maria Theresa thaler hindered adoption of some better forms of currency.

Our final example of excess inertia comes from the United States in the 1860s. As described earlier, until 1863, all the banknotes in circulation were provided by private banks under individual state banking laws. Counterfeiting was rampant, and occasionally banks were failing, rendering notes useless, or redeemed at very high discount. In 1863 banks started issuing notes under new legislation, the National Banking Act. Those so-called "national banks" were still private banks, usually with a single brick-and-mortar location. But the notes they issued were of a distinct, uniform design, which made it easier to control against counterfeits. Moreover, the national banknotes were insured, which meant that even if the bank failed, the notes would be fully redeemed for specie.

Given that national banks' notes carried less risk than state banks' notes did, they were more reliable money. When passing the law, the government expected that with such an advantage, national banknotes would naturally become widely accepted, rendering state banknotes obsolete. However, after two years there was no visible decline in the use of state banknotes. Since bank failures occurred only occasionally, people may have considered the risk a natural part of the transaction costs, and were not actively looking to minimize those costs. They may have been distrustful of the unfamiliar design and may not have been fully aware of the benefits of the national banknotes. State banknotes were more familiar, and people knew they were accepted in their immediate environment. So state banknotes kept being accepted because everyone expected they'd be accepted.

The government effectively put an end to state banknotes by putting a 10 percent tax on banks paying the state banknotes out over the counter, even if they were the bank's own notes.[22] This finally ended the era of state banking.

2.3.4. Coexistence of Various Currencies

Despite the winner-take-all dynamics, and despite excess inertia, sometimes different forms of money, different currencies, can coexist in the economy. This happens when the different currencies serve different purposes.

We have the first records of silver used as money from ancient Mesopotamia. It replaced an older type of money—barley. Metal held a higher value than barley did: a piece of silver was worth more than the same volume of barley.[23] This is why silver was more convenient for transactions involving large values and longer distances (e.g., a shipload of products). For everyday local exchanges of much smaller values, metals were too valuable. Those trades were still conducted using barley. Thus, even though metal was handier and was adopted throughout Mesopotamia, winner-take-all dynamics have not lead to metal money pushing out older barley money completely.

Similarly, the introduction of coins has not completely eliminated the use of unminted metal in transactions, especially high value ones, where a large number of standardized coins would be unhandy. Different transactions have different "needs," and different currencies may coexist if they serve these different needs better. There are still costs of parallel money—exchanging barley for metal and vice versa, but the benefits of matching functionality to needs may be worth the costs. The two types of money serve their respective purposes better than having only one type.

We can also think of contemporary banknotes and coins as two different kinds of currency that coexist because they serve different purposes. We tend to use banknotes and coins for different types of transactions. Typically, we use coins for small-value transactions and banknotes for large-value ones. Sure, there is overlap, but if we only had banknotes or only coins, trades would be more laborious. And for their respective roles, the two types utilize optimal technology.[24] Banknotes of very small denominations that circulate very frequently would wear out too quickly. Coins are more durable, but they are heavier than banknotes are. Using many coins, even of higher denominations, for large-value transactions would be less handy than using bills of the same denominations. Customers would need to carry fewer coins if more denominations were available. For that to work, merchants would need to have all denominations always available, and with a larger number of denominations, they would need to tie up more of their capital just to have change ready. The transaction costs would also increase because one would need to search for coins among more denominations.

These different roles that coins and banknotes play were apparent from the time banknotes were introduced. For example, some of the first banknotes issued by the Bank of England in the eighteenth century were the ten-pound and twenty-pound notes. These quantities, equivalent to roughly a thousand dollars nowadays, limited the use of the banknotes to the richest strata of society. Not surprisingly, they were used almost exclusively for large-value business transactions and were particularly popular among the financial elites of the City of London.[25]

Overall, we can summarize the competitive forces as follows. There are costs to multiple currencies, including not only the cognitive costs but also the cost of exchange. Different currencies are available—some may be better or worse than others for a particular purpose, and some may be equivalent. People are willing to use multiple currencies and bear the cost of compatibility and exchange if the currencies serve different purposes and if each is better for its purpose than others are. But people would rather use one currency for a given purpose: network effects matter for currencies. Network effects tilt the economy toward winner-take-all outcomes, where a single currency accounts for all transactions in the economy. In such cases, the incumbent currency may hinder competition, with inertia keeping people from adopting new (or multiple) currencies that could improve their well-being.

2.4. VIRTUAL MONEY?

Our overview of the history of money brings us to modern times and to the main focus of this book: digital currencies. The background we covered in this chapter will give us a better understanding of these innovations and will help us highlight the similarities between them and earlier stages in the evolution of money. This is perhaps most apparent in the widely used terms "virtual money" and "virtual currency." Many of the historical examples of money deserve to be called virtual, starting with the very first system of exchange based on collective memory.

One could perhaps think about this collective memory-based system among the hunter-gatherers as the very first virtual currency. The "currency" was virtual in that it captured many of the functions money plays nowadays, even though it did not physically exist.[26] People could earn the currency by doing favors for others or providing goods and services to others. Each person's "savings" were held in the collective memory, which became the equivalent of a bank account or transactions leger.

"Virtual" is often used as a substitute for "digital." Even this, however, is a broad description that may capture more than is intended. For example, funds in a bank account are stored electronically, so they can be thought about as "digital money"—although, because they are just a digitized version of the government-issued money, they are not "digital currency."

In the remaining chapters, we will now focus on digital currencies, understood as money in a digital form that has no physical counterpart and that usually has its own unit of account. Currently, those currencies can be also seen as play and fringe money, in the sense of operating at the fringes of the economy. We will analyze the economic forces behind their development and compare them with traditional money that is nowadays almost exclusively issued by governments. On the basis of this analysis, we will also peek into the future of digital currencies.

CHAPTER 3

PLATFORM-BASED CURRENCIES

In recent years, many large Internet companies have introduced their own digital currencies. Most of these companies run large platforms that span media, entertainment, and e-commerce. The market has seen Amazon Coins, Facebook Credits, Q-coins, Microsoft Points, and Reddit gold, to only name a few. This is on top of the many video games and gaming platforms that have their own currencies—for example, World of Warcraft gold, Second Life's Linden dollars, or Eve Online's Interstellar Kredits. All of these currencies have been introduced by large online platforms that, in one way or another, help interactions between their large groups of diverse members: buyers and sellers, game players, or simply people who want to exchange pictures and messages with one another. These interactions often involve some form of trade that may be helped by a special, custom-built, currency that online platforms provide for the convenience of their members. It is important to see that in all these cases, the currency is entirely controlled by the platform, which can set all of its features and properties. In this chapter, we review a few such "centrally controlled" currencies to understand the key drivers of their design and the rules governing their use.

Special-purpose money centrally introduced and controlled by various organizations, from commercial entities to local or national government organizations, is not entirely new. For example, casino chips and Monopoly money have been around for a century. Also, while they are rarely called currencies, the world has been quite used to airline miles redeemable for future flights, hotel reservations, or car rentals. Airline miles are just one example of the family of loyalty programs in millions of stores or for a multitude of products and services. Governments have regularly introduced or allowed for private introduction of actual currencies restricted to specific social groups, geographic regions, or product categories. For example, there are a number of local currencies functioning in different regions of the United States, for example, Ithaca Hours in upstate New York or BerkShares in western Massachusetts. Food stamps are another example of special-purpose money: they are essentially a payment system restricted to use by the poor and only for certain products.

What has changed, however, is that the digital era offers vast new opportunities and challenges for the introduction and use of special-purpose currencies. First, the digital nature of these currencies provides endless opportunities for the design of new features adapted to the specific needs of the business introducing them. As we will see below, these varied needs may explain many of the differences between today's platform-based currencies. Also, besides the multiplicity of features, the digital era also makes it much more cost effective to monitor and restrict the use of the currency. Most important, however, many of the recently introduced digital currencies are *global*. The organizations offering them are often large platforms, spanning across many nations. As such, these currencies may have a global impact. This fact did not escape the attention of policy makers and economic commentators. Matthew Yglesias (2012), mentioned earlier, worried about Facebook Credits taking on established state-issued currencies, and his worries were echoed by economists who saw the coincidence of these currency introductions with the rise of developed countries' national debt after the financial crisis as particularly threatening for state-issued currencies. Similar concerns were expressed when Amazon introduced Amazon Coins in 2013. Experts saw a potential for these currencies to challenge central banks' monopoly on issuing money. Besides the historical context of the financial crisis, these concerns were also fueled by the fact that Facebook and Amazon are large platforms with a broad international reach and very large customer base. Amazon has an estimated 250 million customers, and Facebook has well exceeded a billion members, not even counting the fact that it owns additional large online platforms, such as Instagram and WhatsApp. One is often reminded that with its size, if Facebook were a country, it would count as the third most populous, after China and India.

By now, these concerns have largely disappeared, not only because Facebook decided to abandon Facebook Credits. As we will argue below, neither Facebook Credits nor Amazon Coins had the real potential to become widely accepted currencies despite the large size of their patron companies. The main reason is that these currencies are severely limited in their functionality. For example, neither Facebook Credits nor Amazon Coins can be transferred to other users, and they can only be spent on Facebook or Amazon. Amazon Coins have additional restrictions on what they can be spent on—only on selected apps on Amazon Kindle Fire. With such limitations, they could not become a means of payment rivaling the dollar, euro, or yen. Indeed, transferability is necessary, although not sufficient attribute for a platform-based currency to have a wider impact. Yet, platforms may find it in their best interest to limit this functionality.[1]

To be fair, commentators' concerns were somewhat justified. First, some platforms did introduce currencies with full functionalities that can be freely exchanged for state-issued currencies; for example, Second Life's Linden dollars can be exchanged back and forth between US dollars. While these currencies had no major influence on state-issued currencies so far, this is largely due to the fact that the underlying platforms failed to grow large enough for such impact. Moreover, even limited local currencies may represent a challenge for regulators who will find it hard to coordinate across national borders to implement regulation. Yet, with the flexibility in design that the digital nature of these currencies makes possible, such regulation might be increasingly necessary.

What drives this design? To understand the larger picture of digital currencies, we need to examine more carefully the incentives of Internet companies when issuing their currencies. Special-purpose or "local" currencies have always been introduced with specific objectives in mind. Their design closely reflects these objectives while trying to avoid unintended consequences. This has been the case for non-digital local currencies as well, as we will illustrate below. Among our digital examples, Amazon and Facebook had already grown large before introducing their currencies. They operate according to their specific business models, and their spectacular growth may be an indicator that these business models are successful. We venture the hypothesis that the companies only introduce their currencies if it reinforces their business models. The main insight is that digitization allows for the *design* of currencies to an unprecedented extent, and companies are designing their currencies by choosing the currency's attributes in such a way as to best match their business models.[2]

In what follows, we first review a few classic examples of centrally introduced local currencies and show how their design features reflect the underlying objectives of the organizations that have introduced them. Next, we look at four typical business models of large Internet platforms and analyze how the features of their recently introduced digital currencies reflect these business models. Finally, we discuss the limits to the distinction that can be made between platform-based currencies and state-issued money and discuss the challenges that large-scale digital currencies might represent.

In our analysis of the following examples, we will focus on three main attributes, which can be easily set and controlled by the entity introducing the currency. Arguably, these attributes have a major impact on whether the currency can facilitate trade (a currency's core purpose) and in what specific context it can do so.[3] The first such attribute is *acquirability*, or how the currency can be acquired. The designer of the currency can, for example, require that the currency only be "earned" with certain specific activities or that it can be "bought" (exchanged for) other currencies or goods. The second feature that we examine is *transferability*, or what the restrictions are, if any, on transferring the currency to others. Typically, the question is whether it can be transferred to other members on the platform. Finally, the third feature, *redeemability*, prescribes what the currency can buy. In particular, of central interest is whether it can be exchanged for state-issued currency. In other words, redeemability defines the restrictions on spending the currency. If a currency does not have restrictions in any of the attributes—that is, it can be bought and earned, can be transferred to anyone participating in the system, can be exchanged for state-issued currency, and can be spent on anything within the system—we call such currency *fully equipped*. State-issued currencies can be considered fully equipped currencies, at least within the country whose government issued them. Most digital currencies, however, are typically restricted in one or multiple attributes. Those restrictions are deliberately put in place in order to reinforce the business model of the issuing platform. Let us consider several examples in more detail, starting with some traditional ones, rooted in the non-digital world.

3.1. SPECIAL CURRENCIES OF THE OFF-LINE WORLD

As mentioned earlier, the design of money has been around for a while. All kinds of loyalty points, food stamps, and some of the banking products are examples of such design. Below, we will look at three particular examples— BerkShares, food stamps, and mortgages—to analyze the design challenges that they have faced in light of their issuers' objectives.

BerkShares
BerkShares were introduced in 2006 in the Berkshires region of Massachusetts with the intention to help the local population in a touristy area. The presence of tourists increased prices in the area but not necessarily local wages. Some local businesses got together and agreed to give a discount to the local population—in essence, introducing an effective price discrimination scheme. This was done through BerkShares, a local paper currency. You could get BerkShares at a local bank paying 95 US cents per one BerkShare. But the participating businesses accept them on par with the dollar.

Since they are a paper currency, any restriction on transferring them between local and nonlocal people would be too costly to enforce. Moreover, when you use BerkShares, you do not need to prove that you are a local, or even pretend to be local. One could imagine a requirement that you need to show your driver's license with a local address to use BerkShares. But this may be too burdensome or elicit negative sentiment from tourists, and may slow down transactions. Since you can only use them at participating businesses, BerkShares have restrictions on where one can spend them but not on who can spend them. Anyone can buy them at a local bank. They aren't advertised, so not many people know about them. But, of course, locals would be more likely to know about them. This has been probably the only barrier for everyone taking advantage of the discount. Surely, if too many tourists were to take advantage of BerkShares, one can easily imagine additional restrictions on acquiring and spending BerkShares. Since they would be costly to implement, in the additional time and burden it takes to complete transactions, they wouldn't be implemented until there was a need to do so. In contrast, for digital currencies, such restrictions are much less likely to bear these additional transaction costs. They could be incorporated in the design right from the start.

Food Stamps

Food stamps are another example of designed money, one where restrictions on spending are actually in effect. You can only spend them in particular places, on particular products—only on food and not on alcohol or tobacco. The purpose of food stamps is for the government to provide food to families with low incomes. Giving such families the same funds in cash would enable them to spend that money on goods other than food, including drugs or alcohol. This would go against the purpose of the program. Introducing a distinct currency with restriction on its use allows the government to achieve its goal—supplementing food to those families in need. Originally, food stamps had the form of paper stamps or coupons, similar to paper currency. They were accepted by participating food stores no matter who was using them. That meant that there was no restriction on transferring them—eligible families could pass their food stamps to noneligible families—and no restrictions on who could spend them. Their use was only restricted by where they could be spent and on what products. Since the late 1990s, the paper stamps were phased out and replaced by a debit-card system called Electronic Benefit Transfer (EBT) administered by banks, presumably to save costs. In 2008, the government changed the name from Food Stamp Program to Supplemental Nutrition Assistance Program. EBT cards are name based, and the government delivers the new balance to the eligible person's card. There is still no particular restriction on who can use the card to make purchases, as there is no requirement of checking IDs. Since the benefits are given to the household, this arrangement allows different member of the household to pick up the food. Nonetheless, transferring the benefit to someone else became more burdensome. You cannot simply hand another person $5 worth of food stamps. If you hand over your card, you will part not only with the whole balance but also the future benefits.

Mortgages

A mortgage can also be thought of as a currency with a spending restriction. (Funny, we usually don't think about food stamps and mortgages in the same category.) You get a credit from the bank. Typically, you cannot take this money and go shopping or go on vacation.[4] Generally, you can only spend it on a particular piece of real estate. Moreover, the mortgage cannot be easily transferred—it is restricted to a single entity, usually a person or a couple. Generally, there are also further restrictions in using a mortgage: since the collateral is often the specific real estate in question, the mortgage holder may be required to provide some insurance for the property. There may be specific payment schedules imposed and penalties for late and/or early payment. Clearly, a mortgage is a quite complex form of payment.

*   *   *

In all three of the above examples, the special-money system has been introduced by an entity—a consortium of shoppers, the government, or a bank, respectively—with specific objectives in mind. The rules governing the currencies create particular incentives for the members of the target population. The design features of these private currencies need to take into account these incentives in order to support the entity's objectives. This often means carefully considering trade-offs. For example, in the case of food stamps, the government realized that it needed to restrict transferability to make sure that only the target social group benefits from the subsidies. Too much restriction on transferability (e.g., providing access only to the head of household), however, makes the use of the subsidy impractical because it is often family members who are in charge of shopping. The EBT debit-card solution is a good compromise in this case. Another important consideration in the choice of features for a currency is the cost of implementing the features. Most of the time, these costs are not trivial, no matter who bears them. The bank fees charged for the management of the EBT cards absorb some of the value of the food stamps, so using EBT cards to restrict transferability has a cost both to the currency's issuer and, indirectly, to the user.

In what follows, we argue that digital currencies provide much more flexibility in introducing design features and make the monitoring of their corresponding restrictions much less costly. This should mean that the type of businesses capable of introducing digital currencies effectively could use this flexibility to their advantage. Nonetheless, the change that digital currencies bring is quantitative rather than qualitative. It is not a completely new thing but rather a change in degree. Yet, we should not dismiss it because of insufficient novelty. It can still have a very large impact. Email is an example of such a quantitative, not qualitative, change that has nonetheless significantly impacted our work and life in general, creating a more connected and "just-in-time" work place. Email is just quicker mail. Instead of days, we get mail electronically within minutes or less. In the beginning, people checked their email once in a while and wrote emails similar to traditional letters. (Remember when you needed to connect via dial-up to collect your email, maybe once every few days?) Quickly, however, messages were more frequently returned and got shorter. Internet connections got better, and now we usually send short, informal messages all the time and receive them almost instantly. Email turned from a digital version of letters into digital version of notes passed in a class. Similarly, who knows where the proliferation of differentiated digital currencies may take us?

As the examples above demonstrate, in exploring more recent private digital currency systems, we need to keep in mind that such systems are driven by the interplay between the objectives of the entities introducing them and the incentives that they provide for the users. In turn, in the case of private companies like Internet platforms, the objectives are driven by these companies' business models. It is not surprising then that fundamentally different business models lead to private currencies with very different design features.

3.2. PLATFORM-BASED CURRENCIES IN THE DIGITAL ERA

The digital era offers an unprecedented extent to which currency design may be controlled. In certain cases, technology has also significantly reduced the cost of implementing alternative designs. In particular, technology can easily adjust the three fundamental design features we have reviewed above. It allows one, for example, to easily control to whom the currency can or cannot be transferred (transferability). Technology can also better control how the currency can be acquired (acquirability) and how it can be spent (redeemability). Table 3.1 provides a few possible design combinations that have been implemented by some digital platform businesses. Using the design elements that we have discussed above, it summarizes a few observable combinations of these features in businesses. As can be seen from the table, these three characteristics differentiate various platform-based digital currencies observed in the real world.

Importantly, each of these three features provides a few specific incentives for their users. For example, if the currency cannot be redeemed for state-issued currency but can only be "spent" on the platform, then this reinforces customer captivity or customer loyalty: leaving the platform means leaving assets behind. Surely, it is better to

Table 3.1 Design attributes of platform-based currencies

Acquire	Transfer	Cash out	Environment
Buy only	No	No	A "wallet" to store cash to be spent on the platform only (e.g., PlayStation Store Wallet). It often facilitates the administration of a promotion (e.g., Amazon Coin).
Buy only	Yes	No	A wallet combined with a trading system, but still only in-platform (e.g., Steam gaming platform).
Buy only	No	Yes	A simple wallet that may only be relevant if there is a need to trigger micropayments (not observed in platform-based currencies).
Buy only	Yes	Yes	A payment system that does not require a separate currency (e.g., PayPal or Venmo).
Earn	Yes	Yes	A promotion device to encourage people to try the product (not observed in platform-based currencies).
Earn	No	Yes	A job market (e.g., Amazon's Mechanical Turk).
Earn only	No	No	Not really a currency, but it may be a display of status (e.g., DKP in WoW, karma in Guild Wars 2).
Earn	Yes	No	A fully functioning virtual economy with no direct cash out; one can indirectly cash out and buy because a transfer is possible (e.g., WoW gold).
Earn or buy	Yes	Yes	A fully functioning virtual economy (e.g., Second Life).
Earn or buy	No	No	A wallet combined with promotional incentives (e.g., Facebook Credits).

use these assets to consume more on the platform than to lose them. This, of course, is beneficial for the platform particularly if its business model is based on usage intensity. This is why many of the digital platforms (e.g., World of Warcraft or Facebook) restrict cashing-out by simply not making it possible to convert their currencies into state-issued currency. At the same time, restricting funds within the platform may also mean that people might be less inclined to inject funds from outside into the platform in the first place. If such "investments" are critical, say for the development of the platform itself, then this consideration needs to be traded off against customer loyalty. This is the case for the virtual world Second Life, which entirely relies on its users to build all the content on the platform from the texture of the land to plants, houses, and any object one can imagine.

Among the three key features, transferability is a particularly subtle one. On the one hand, transferability is clearly needed if the platform wants economic interaction between the members. However, transferability creates a possibility for some people to use the platform to earn money and export it from the platform, even if the platform does not officially allow such "cashing-out." As we analyze the case of World of Warcraft gold below, it will become apparent that allowing transferability is generally in conflict with strong restrictions on taking funds out of the platform.

What might explain which design features would be implemented for the currency of a particular platform? Based on the examples and the discussion above, we see that the platforms' business model has a decisive role in the choice of features. The platform's business model provides guidance on the incentives that the platform wants to reinforce for its membership base. Clearly, there might be many other, maybe practical, determinants that need to be considered; for example, technological or regulatory constraints. But digital currency—if adopted—should support the firm's business model. The concept of "business model" is quite complex, however. To be more specific, we will focus on two of its key aspects: the way the platform creates value for its customers/members (i.e., its value proposition) and the way the platform captures this value (i.e., its revenue model). We argue that these two aspects of the business model have a strong influence on the choice of design features for the platform's digital currency.

The dynamic evolution of the Internet has spawned many different business models, and the process of experimentation is far from over. Currently, we have identified four particular models that cover a large number of successful digital platform businesses. They are the following:

1. Online, interactive video games, such as World of Warcraft and Diablo
2. Virtual worlds, such as Second Life and Eve Online
3. Social networks, such as Facebook and Tencent
4. Product promotion platforms, such as Amazon's e-reader platform or a gaming platform like Steam

We look at each of these four business models and analyze their digital currency designs. Our goal is to explore how their value creation process and their revenue model are linked to the kind of currencies that they introduced. An important caveat is that what we call "typical" business models exhibit a fair amount of variation themselves. In fact, the strict separation of these four categories is somewhat forced because there are many platforms that sit somewhere between the categories. Online interactive video games have an incredible variety, from relatively simple and stylized ones to complex universes. World of Warcraft, for example, can be legitimately seen as a virtual world rather than simply a video game, depending on one's perspective, and we will need to be more explicit in making this difference clear. On the other hand, Eve Online may be seen as a video game rather than a virtual world. Similarly, Tencent can be legitimately seen as a social network even though it is one of the largest gaming platforms in the world, hosting many of its own games. In what follows, we provide a more precise characterization of these business models, but it is important to keep in mind that any classification is somewhat artificial, given the large number and variety of digital platforms available.

In one important aspect, these platforms are quite similar—they all exhibit some form of consumption externality. In such environments, consumers benefit from other consumers using the same platform. As the main purpose of platforms is to facilitate interactions between groups of consumers, it is quite natural that consumption externalities are present. In turn, the recent emergence of such platforms is not surprising given the Internet's core capacity to connect large number of people. As such, platforms built on the Internet naturally exploit this feature. Let us take the case of video games, for example. Here, the more people play the game, the more enjoyable it is—it results in more thrills and also in more opportunities for collaboration. Similarly, on social networks, more people sharing content means that there is more content to consume. For an individual member sharing his or her content, there is a larger audience if the platform has a larger number of members. In virtual worlds, more members means a richer and more complex world with more objects present and more things to do. While there are differences across platforms in how exactly these externalities play out, they are present in one form or another, naturally leading to network effects. The presence and nature of consumption externalities is often reflected in the design of the currencies the platforms adopt.

Finally, it is important to point out that digital platforms and their currencies are relatively new phenomena, and what we observe today is not the final and definitive form of the digital currencies of these businesses. The experimentation in this domain is far from over. In fact, and most interestingly, some of the currencies introduced did not work out and had to be abandoned or needed a substantial redesign during their short history. These cases are particularly insightful for understanding the link between the digital currencies' design features and their role in the platforms' corresponding business models.

3.2.1. Online Video Games and World of Warcraft Gold

World of Warcraft is the most popular massively multiplayer online role-playing game (MMORPG). Created by Blizzard Entertainment, it has over 8 million gamers interacting with their avatars in this medieval virtual world. As they play, they gain skills and wealth. They go on quests, alone or more commonly in groups, to face challenges and gain even more skills and wealth. The quests are demanding, and it is important for success to build a team with the right composition of complementary skills for the particular challenge. The currency of the realm is World of Warcraft gold (WoW gold). It can be freely transferred between members of the game, but according to the rules of the game, it cannot be acquired in exchange for state-issued currency, nor can it be redeemed for state-issued currency. WoW gold can only be earned in the game and only spent in the game.

It is easy to understand the purpose of most of these design features. Allowing people to earn gold makes them progress in the game. Together with the rule that WoW gold can only be spent in the game, this design creates loyalty. The design is also compatible with firm's revenue model: a monthly membership fee. The earned and locked-in funds boost loyalty to the game. This is all the more important because the game exhibits strong consumption externalities and associated network effects: the more people play the game, the more there are possibilities to form or join teams and complete quests of increased difficulty. In this setup, it makes sense to grow the user base, and this is helped by making the platform sticky for those who have already been hooked. Their presence will make the game all the more attractive for new players who are considering joining.

Transferability is also important for World of Warcraft's value proposition. The game is based on interactions between players by letting them form coalitions to complete quests. Completing a quest is typically rewarded with a bounty. Transferability ensures that the bounty can be appropriately shared across the members of the coalition. This may happen according to skills or contribution to the quest. Transferability also helps members to trade weapons and other objects with one another. This, the trading aspect of the game also reinforces the network effects.

Yet, in one respect, this currency design may seem overly restrictive: WoW gold cannot be bought with state-issued currency, only earned in the game. Why wouldn't Blizzard want to make extra bucks selling WoW gold? Wouldn't it attract even more members? It turns out that this could actually undermine World of Warcraft's value proposition to members and, as a result, Blizzard's revenues. World of Warcraft's revenue comes from gamers' subscriptions. They keep paying as long as the game delivers the high quality satisfaction they have signed up for. As mentioned earlier, interaction with other gamers is crucial in the game. The quests at higher levels require several or even a few dozen of the gamers to collaborate. However, beyond the size of the team, the skills of one's collaborators are also critical for success. Higher level skills are desirable, and skills need to be complementary within the team. Yet, most of the time, when selecting team members for a quest, the gamer does not know the potential candidates well. Fortunately, the status achieved in the game—which can only be guessed from his visible clothing and accessories—is a good proxy for the gamer's skill. A successful quest requires a team with the right mixture of skills. If all status signs are earned by progressing through the game, then status is a good indicator of skill. If, on the other hand, the clothing and accessories were purchased with money earned outside of the game, the displayed status no longer correlates with the skill, and status is then not only uninformative but also actually misleading to the gamers trying to put together a successful quest team. If Blizzard were to change the rules and allow new (therefore unexperienced) gamers to buy status from others, this would create a strong negative externality for the other ("honest") gamers. The presence of such impostors could quickly destroy the game if trust in peer players' skills is broken.

WoW gold is purposefully designed to serve the game's business model. It illustrates how deliberately restricting certain attributes of the currency may help creating value for customers. It is important to realize however that not all interactive games find these restrictions optimal. In particular, a very large proportion of games—most social games on mobile phones, for example—adopt the classic "freemium" model. In the freemium model, one can play for free, earning "credit" (typically some digital currency) when advancing in the game—that is, achieving higher status. Clash of Clans, developed by the game studio Supercell is a good example. It can be played on a PC or on a smartphone. The game is fairly simple. Players own a village and their goal is to develop it as much as possible. Development essentially means building an army with sophisticated weapons and solid defenses against raiders. Funds to build the army come from economic activities of the village, which—with some oversimplification—boil down to digging for gold. Gold in turn can buy more weapons and so on. An interesting part of the game is that one can use its army to raid other villages and steal gold from them. In this way, everyone is fighting, and everyone tries to achieve a better "status," measured as a rank across players, by adjusting their strategies in terms of the investments they make in their armies, defenses, and gold digging technologies. However, players can also buy credit with state-issued currency that will accelerate their advancement by providing them with extra funds. Instead of a fixed subscription fee, it is these purchases, usually coming from a very small proportion of the players, that represent the core revenue source of the game. Clash of Clans is a typical example of a freemium game.

Interestingly, freemium games do not seem to suffer from the fact that some players can buy into "status." In these games, while players can interact in various ways— helping each other, trading with each other, for example— they do not rely so critically on each other's advanced skills. In fact, in Clash of Clans, any partner with a large army is just as good as any other, no matter whether the army was purchased or "earned" via conquests. As such, the value of a partner is not closely linked to experience in the game. In other words, the fact that observed status is not necessarily related to skill does not hurt the other players. Thus, inexperienced players do not create a strong negative externality for others. Freemium games typically also have restrictions on the withdrawal of funds created or purchased in the game—these funds cannot be retrieved for state-issued currency. This restriction keeps players in the game, which also helps other players join. Yet, as we will see below, it is not always easy for the owner of the game to enforce this rule, and some players go out of their way to break it.

Fraud with Digital Currency

While games' digital features are easy to implement and monitor on the platform, the Internet has made it increasingly easy to break the rules using other interactive platforms that facilitate commerce, such as eBay, for instance. In World of Warcraft, for example, despite rules of the game to the contrary, there are a lot of external transfers between players. People are willing to buy WoW gold for state-issued currency—along with items you can buy with gold, like weapons or armor—to advance in the game without the time investment. eBay banned trading of in-game currencies and assets in January 2007,[5] but there are a number of other sites where one can buy WoW gold for state-issued currency.[6] This indicates that there is demand for in-game assets. And these are not only occasional trades. There is so much demand that some people in developing countries turn it into their day job to play a game, collect WoW gold, and then sell it for state-issued currency. This activity is popularly called "gold mining." In extreme cases, it even led to infamous instances of forced gold mining in Chinese labor camps, where the guards made the prisoners play the game by night, selling the proceeds.[7] Clearly, the existence of these "black markets" did not help the reputation of the game. But even without these extreme cases, as we have seen above, black markets hurt the gamers by flooding the platform with people whose status displays did not match their skill, thereby, spoiling the game. Interestingly, World of Warcraft gamers themselves started policing such suspicious behavior and reporting it to the game administrators. As a consequence, Blizzard has expelled several players for fraud, but the practice has not disappeared.

Gamers themselves found a better solution. The problem of "fake players" became so annoying for them that they decided to mostly ignore the traditional displays of status and instead were relying on so-called Dragon Kill Points (DKPs) for the assessment of the skill of a potential quest mate. DKPs are acquired by participating in a quest that kills a particular type of creature, called a *boss*. Initially bosses were mainly dragons, hence the name. The killed creature leaves behind a treasure, or a loot. When there are many people in the quest, they need to agree on how to divide the loot. Games solved this problem by allotting the DKPs to the participants of a successful quest and allowing them to use those points to buy certain items.[8] But DKPs can only buy those items that are rewarded for killing a boss. If a player does not spend their DKPs, they accumulate, and they can be spent later. In other words, DKPs are an alternative currency with restrictions on what the currency can be spent on. What is most important is that DKPs are nontransferable. DKPs have a far more limited use than WoW gold does, and DKPs cannot substitute for WoW gold in its economic role in the game. However, in the presence of black markets for WoW gold, DKPs turned out to be more useful for signaling skill. At first DKPs were informally assigned and tracked within groups of gamers, called guilds, for the purpose of goods allocation. As they gained importance as a skill signaling tool, Blizzard formalized this dual system as a so-called Guild Advancement system aside from the existing gold.

Unsuccessful Experiments and Learning
Blizzard also experimented with a different design of currency systems in other games. Not all experiments were successful. Given the rampant sales of in-game gold and items in the "black market," Blizzard decided to build such functionality directly into the game for the third edition of their popular Diablo game. In this game, a player defeats enemy creatures at an increasing challenge level. At each level, a defeated creature drops weapons (and gold) that help the player defeat a more demanding creature in the future. The culmination of the game is a fight with Diablo, the "lord of terror." The game Diablo is less interactive than World of Warcraft is, but it still has some cooperative elements. A player who has a surplus of one type of weapon, armor, or other items but who needs a different type can trade with other players either directly or through the in-game markets, so called auction houses. The trades could happen by using in-game gold (at Gold Auction Houses), or using state-issued currency (at Real Money Auction Houses). Blizzard charges a transaction fee on such trades, whether they are done with in-game or state-issued currencies. Additionally, Blizzard charges a cash-out fee if a player takes out state-issued money outside of the platform. Unlike World of Warcraft, Diablo is not subscription based. There is only the one-time fee of purchasing the game. Thus, making money on users' cash transactions in and out of the game made sense from the perspective of the revenue model. However, the possibility for inexperienced players to buy status represented an

important problem, even in this game where the level of cooperation, and therefore, the assessment of a partner's skill, is not so critical. The endorsement of state-issued currency trade within the game eliminated outside black markets and made the company earn more revenues, but it also reinforced the negative externalities represented by "fake players." In March 2014, Blizzard closed down the auction houses, saying that the Real Money Auction Houses were detrimental to the game because they "short-circuited" the title and made the game less satisfying.[9]

Blizzard seemed to get a good grip on the problem of currency design in yet another game called Guild Wars 2. In this game, there are three types of currency: gems, gold, and karma. Gems are directly linked to the state-issued money. Players can buy them with state-issued money at a fixed rate. Gold can be earned in the game or bought with gems. However, gold is bought in a player-driven market. That means that the gems-gold exchange rate is not set by the platform. Instead, the rate depends on the relative supplies of and demand for gold and gems. Karma, on the other hand, is earned through game tasks and cannot be bought or transferred. Most microtransactions and in-game purchases, whether from the platform or directly between players, occur in fully transferable gold. But karma is used to buy unique awards. Thus, while gold and gems can be used to adorn the avatars and the players' environment, only rewards bought with nontransferable karma directly signal the player's skill.

These examples of Blizzard games show the importance of transferability for the currency. Transferability makes it easier to bypass other restrictions, such as restrictions on buy-in and cash-out, if users find it beneficial to do so. If it is important for the value of the platform that the users do not buy the currency, as in the case of skill signaling in

World of Warcraft and Guild Wars 2, the platform needs to rely on a currency that is not transferable. This may create conflict if, at the same time, one of the attractions of the activity on the platform is economic interactions between users. These economic activities on the platform usually require a transferable currency. As Blizzard's example shows, one possible solution is a dual system that allows for buying the transferable currency, formalizing a de facto state, while also operating a separate nontransferable currency earned in the game and thus signaling skill.[10]

3.2.2. Virtual Worlds and Linden Dollars

The previous examples looked at restricting currency functions. But the optimal design for some platform businesses may point to a fully equipped currency. An example of such an unrestricted currency is the Linden dollar, the currency used in a virtual world called Second Life. At this point, it is important to ask, what is the difference between a "virtual world" and a complex video game such as World of Warcraft? The short answer is that virtual worlds are "MMORPGs without purpose." Classic MMORPGs represent a well-defined world with well-defined rules and a consistent visual appearance. Most important, they have well-defined goals for their players. Players face specific quests, there is a known hierarchy among them, and everyone knows what needs to be done to achieve the goals. In Second Life, very little is defined. One can choose to do whatever one wants, and people end up doing wildly different things. These can be very complex activities, such as running a virtual bar (with virtual drinks and real music mixed by a DJ, represented of course by his or her avatar), building and selling sophisticated spaceships, or operating a gallery with beautiful paintings. In contrast, activities can also be really simple and not requiring as much effort, such as hanging out with friends (maybe in a bar), decorating one's avatar, just visiting locations in the virtual world, and so on. In fact, the virtual world itself is undefined as well—one can visit entirely different universes and meet avatars with very different looks. In one region, for instance, some members have rebuilt the entire universe of the movie *Avatar*, with floating islands and spectacular vegetation. Other regions were built to look like abandoned industrial wasteland. Every aspect of the environment, from the shape of the land to the vegetation, buildings, creatures, and so on, needs to be built from scratch by the members of the virtual world.[11]

Second Life is probably the most extreme of virtual worlds in that almost nothing is defined in it—it provides unlimited possibilities. In this sense, it is the opposite of World of Warcraft, which is a fully codified virtual world. Virtual worlds represent a continuum between these extremes, with many platforms sitting somewhere in the middle. Eve Online, for example, is a utopian virtual world inspired by Ayn Rand's ideas of a libertarian universe. While it also allows almost unlimited freedom to its members, the environment is somewhat more defined than is Second Life's. In one respect, however, Eve Online is "freer" than Second Life is: it has no property rights enforced by the platform. Instead, members need to get organized to enforce these. In Second Life, property rights are well policed by the game, and only by hacking the platform can someone steal virtual property from others.

Given this freedom, there will be many different people on the platform with wildly differing tastes and very different activities. In fact, virtual worlds are built to be fully functional economies. This means that these platforms have many opportunities to collect revenues from their members. A general tax on economic activity seems to be a good way to collect revenues. In the case of Second Life, where the world would be virtually empty without the objects built by residents, a good proxy for economic activity is land ownership, as it only makes sense to pay for it if something is built on the land. Taxing virtual land is aligned with the platform's cost of serving customers, as more land and more objects on the land mean more memory used by the platform's information technology system.

It is not surprising then that Second Life's revenue model is tightly linked to economic activity on the platform. Specifically, the model has three main revenue sources. First, it collects revenues from "advanced" users, who have the right to build things. Essentially, it charges a membership fee. Second, Second Life also collects revenues from sales of virtual land. A small island can be purchased for a one-time payment of about $1,000 followed by a continuous rent, usually around $200. Finally, Second Life collects a transaction fee from the exchange between Linden dollars and state-issued currency. All of these revenues are broadly linked to the diverse economic activities on the platform.

Second Life's currency, the Linden dollar, is a fully equipped currency. It can be earned within the platform, usually by working for someone, but it can also be purchased with state-issued currency. It can be transferred to anyone or spent within the platform to purchase anything that is for sale. Finally, it can also be changed back to state-issued currency and taken out of the platform. This last feature is somewhat puzzling. Why does Second Life allow people to take out their money from the platform? As we have seen before, this may encourage people to leave the platform either because, simply, there is no cost in leaving when one wants to try other things or because people may want to "cash out" after having been successful. Clearly, this does not necessarily benefit Second Life, especially in view of the strong, positive consumption externalities present for virtual worlds. Why allow it then? In short, the "cash-out" policy has to do with the provision of incentives to "invest" in the platform by building content in it. If Linden Labs, the owner of Second Life, wants to have a vibrant interactive community on the platform, including a complex economy, it needs to provide incentives for people to invest, and this is for a very heterogeneous membership base. First, people need to build things. For complex objects, such as a plane, a musical instrument, or a shopping center, building might require collaboration of multiple people or a combination of multiple elements already available from others. Since common pre-designed "quests" are not available, collaboration often necessitates hiring of labor. Furthermore, just as in the real world, to function well in Second Life, extensive trade is needed. Most complex objects require large investments of time. It is unreasonable to expect that everyone can spend this time in the game, so the platform needs to encourage investment in terms of money. For all practical purposes, Second Life is like a real economy, with investment, labor, and product markets and clear property rights. Indeed, it has been pointed out that one of the reasons why users were willing to build a large variety of things to populate the virtual world was that, very early on, the platform declared that the residents (as Second Life users are called) owned the virtual assets they created in the game, and residents could freely sell these assets.

In this sense, Second Life is not a game like the MMOR-PGs we have reviewed above. By 2008, many of its residents moved part of their professional lives to Second Life, earning Linden dollars by building things, opening and running stores, or simply working for other virtual businesses. Accordingly, the Internal Revenue Service declared that earnings in Linden dollars were taxable and many other governments made similar announcements. While for most people these earnings were ephemeral, some people made a real fortune selling digital goods on Second Life.[12] Many real-world businesses—from retailers such as American Apparel, media companies such as Reuters to, maybe more naturally, technology companies like Sun Microsystems—decided to build a presence on Second Life. They were followed by other organizations—schools, universities, and local or national governments—starting serious activities in the virtual world with the hope that it would eventually become a dominant Internet platform.[13]

Eve Online
The virtual world Eve Online, mentioned earlier, is also a typical virtual world in that little is defined for its members, who can freely choose their activities. Eve Online's science-fiction outer space setting is more defined then that of Second Life's. But the platform's members' activities add up to a fairly complex economy that, in many respects, is even more free than is Second Life's. As mentioned earlier, property rights are not enforced centrally, and instead, members need to get organized to protect their property by hiring guards and so on. Eve Online is more "market driven" than Second Life is, in the sense that trade—as opposed to user-generated content—constitutes a more important part of the game. While there are more constraints on creating virtual goods in Eve Online, trade is more complex and requires special skills acquired in the game. Essentially, it relates to the ability of the trader to see more

arbitrage opportunities than do other players who may have invested in developing other skills, such as fighting or building. All these small differences between Eve Online and Second Life, however, do not really matter for the big picture, namely that both platforms run a complex economy. Consequently, both virtual worlds need to provide investment incentives for their members. Accordingly, it is not surprising that Eve Online also has a fully equipped currency, denominated in Interstellar Kredits. It is abbreviated as ISK, which is somewhat confusing, not just because the Icelandic krona is also abbreviated as ISK but because Eve Online's developing company, CCP Games, is based in Reykjavik as well.

Impact Outside of the Platform
While both Second Life and Eve Online have introduced fully equipped currencies—there are no restrictions on buying, earning, gifting or transferring them or even changing them back to state-issued currency—neither Linden dollars nor ISK have had significant impact outside of their respective platforms. Probably, the main reason is that neither platform managed to attract a very large community. There are over 20 million Second Life accounts registered, but it is estimated that about 600,000 of those represent active players. Eve Online's gaming population is estimated at 30,000–40,000 players. Clearly, these numbers are dwarfed by over a billion members on Facebook, for instance.

Yet, early commentators were mostly worried about the fact that virtual worlds' currencies were fully equipped, thereby having the potential to replace state-issued currencies. However, it is misguided to be concerned about the impact of the currency outside the intended platform just because it is fully equipped. As Fung and Halaburda

(2014) show, the currency does not need to be fully equipped to have a potential for impact outside of the platform. It only needs to be transferable. Once transferable, the restrictions around acquirability and redeemability can be manipulated by the users. This was the case for WoW gold, which was broadly traded outside of the World of Warcraft platform despite lacking some key features that Linden dollars had.

With full transferability, if users want to acquire or redeem the currency for state-issued currency, they can find a way for mixed trade, where one part of the transaction takes place on the platform, and the other, outside it. Once the currency is traded outside of the platform, it could be used for trades other than those intended by the platform. Whether it will have an impact outside of the platform crucially depends on whether users have an incentive to use it instead of other available currencies. Thus, this becomes a typical issue of currency competition, which precedes the digital age. There may be some countries where people prefer to use US dollars instead of the local currency. Argentina is often pointed out as one of them. At the same time, currencies that satisfy their role coexist; for example, US and Canadian dollars. Even though there are no restrictions, Canadians have no need to use US dollars in Canada, and Americans have no need to use Canadian dollars in the United States. The same forces play out with digital currencies. Even with transferability, currencies only become adopted outside of the platform if they serve some functions better than existing alternatives do. As far as we know, this hardly happens for WoW gold or for Linden dollars. But there is one well-recorded example where this did take place: Q-coins, the currency of Tencent, a Chinese social network, which we present later in this chapter.

3.2.3. Social Networks and Facebook Credits

Social networks are the third prototypical business model that has emerged for Internet platforms. On these large platforms with hundreds of millions of users, members interact mostly by sharing content with one another. The revenue model is usually advertising based, although there have been other sources of revenues that may provide significant contributions, for example, revenues from app developers or game developers.[14] Facebook is by far the largest social network in the world, with close to 1.5 billion active users. It also owns a variety of other leading social platforms that are more or less connected to Facebook, such as Instagram, WhatsApp, or Facebook Messenger. It is important to realize that Facebook is not simply a platform for its members to interact with user generated content. It is a so-called multisided platform, where a lot of the content is provided by third parties, be it media sites, game or app developers, or simply product brands. Common categories of this third party content consist of videos, articles, and games.

In 2009, Facebook introduced Facebook Credits, which by 2011 became the mandatory currency for all apps and games on the Facebook platform that wanted to charge members. Facebook Credit used non-US dollar denominations and essentially functioned as a virtual wallet. You could add funds online or purchase gift cards at big box stores. The system has since been retired in 2013 in favor of a payment system directly using state-issued currencies.

As mentioned earlier, Facebook Credits could not be transferred between Facebook users. They also could not be exchanged for state-issued currency, such as dollars, euros, or yen. The Credits could be spent on anything on Facebook, whether the content was directly provided by Facebook or by a third party developer, as long as developers accepted Facebook Credits. Between 2009 and 2011, developers could charge users either in Facebook Credits or state-issued currencies. From 2011 until 2013, developers no longer had a choice and had to use Facebook Credits if they wanted to charge users.

In terms of acquirability, users could buy Facebook Credits using state-issued currencies. The price was about 10 Facebook Credits per US dollar, with a number of quantity discounts; for example, for $10 there was a 5 percent bonus, and one received 105 Facebook Credits. Users could also *earn* Facebook Credits, for example by testing a game or taking a survey. Gans and Halaburda (2015) show how restricting the currency's functionality in such a way was optimal for Facebook. The key here is the fact that Facebook's main source of revenue is advertising. The advertising revenue is directly related to the time users spend on the platform. Facebook Credits were optimally designed to induce users to spend more time on the platform.

An important driving force comes from the fact that "consumption" of Facebook exhibits consumption complementarities. That is, the more time my friends spend on Facebook, writing posts and commenting on my photos, the more fun for me it is to spend time on Facebook, posting photos and commenting on their posts. This in turn gives rise to positive network effects—the more people are active on Facebook, the more utility one gets from spending time on Facebook. As we saw, this is a very common property for Internet companies and a very valuable one. If Facebook can induce one user to spend more time on the platform, that user will have a multiplier effect due to these consumption complementarities, and will induce other people to spend more time and maybe attract new people to join Facebook.

Facebook Credits were designed to entice users to spend more time on the platform by giving users a way to enhance their Facebook experience. For example, with Facebook Credits, users could send virtual flowers to a friend or could gain additional options in a game; for example, buy fertilizer for virtual plants to increase the harvest in their virtual farm, get better feed for their virtual pet, and so on. All these activities made spending time on Facebook more pleasurable and thus induced people to spend more time. By allowing both buying and earning, Facebook made sure that Facebook Credits were accessible to both users who had more money than time on their hands (cash-rich) and those who had more time than money (time-rich).

In turn, allowing for transfers between users or exchanging Facebook Credits for state-issued currency would only undermine this objective. Allowing the exchange of Facebook Credits for state-issued currency would allow users to sell earned Facebook Credits back to Facebook. Allowing for transfers between the users could result in a situation where time-rich users earn and sell Facebook Credits to cash-rich users. To make sure that cash-rich users would prefer to buy their Facebook Credits from them rather than from Facebook directly, time-rich users could charge a lower price than Facebook's official rate. Consequently, time-rich users would sell Facebook Credits instead of using them to increase their own Facebook activity. While users often spend time on Facebook when earning Facebook Credits, the credits earning presence mostly does not contribute to advertising revenue. Moreover, if time-rich users do not spend more time on Facebook activities, Facebook is losing the multiplier effect of attracting other users to spend more time. Thus, equipping Facebook Credits with transferability would be less beneficial for Facebook.

Why Were Facebook Credits Shut Down?

Interestingly, Facebook Credits were phased out at the end of 2013. Was it because they were badly designed? From Facebook's perspective, not necessarily. Certainly, at their introduction, users complained at the added level of complexity. Many of the Facebook apps already had their own currencies. For example, Zynga, a large game developer, had zCoin as its internal currency that could be used across Zynga games. After Facebook Credits became mandatory for apps to use, users needed to exchange their dollars for Facebook Credits, and then exchange Facebook Credits for zCoins or FarmVille Dollars. Facebook tried to push the app developers to use Facebook Credits as in-app currency, but only had very limited success. App developers like Zynga preferred their own currencies, because this locked users to their particular app. Facebook Credits, conversely, could be moved between apps. Many of these apps were games that, as we saw above, cared a great deal about consumer loyalty. In other words, by requiring all apps to use Facebook Credits, Facebook made consumer switching between Facebook apps easier. This way Facebook created increased competition for its app developers.

More competition between app developers could have been a good thing for Facebook members. With lower switching costs, this could have encouraged users to consume more content on Facebook, which in turn would have led to even more advertising revenue, and so on. However, this argument does not take into account that Facebook is a multisided platform. To create a healthy ecosystem of apps, it needs to provide sufficient incentives for app developers to invest in quality content. If too little surplus can be captured by app developers then they may seek revenues elsewhere, leaving Facebook and, overall, contributing less content to the platform. Zynga, for example, has been one of the largest developers of Facebook games and for a long time was the largest source of Facebook's revenue. However, Zynga as well as most other game developers had their own platforms that operated outside Facebook. Interestingly, the same reasoning that made Facebook Credits beneficial for Facebook prevented app developers switching from their own currencies to Facebook Credits.

Tencent's Q-coin

Tencent is a Chinese social network. While it serves a similar role as Facebook does in the West, Tencent differs from Facebook in many ways. Until 2014, its revenues were coming mostly from the sales of digital goods that people use to build avatars, decorate their page, play games, or give digital gifts to each other. Compared to Western social networks, Tencent relies less on advertising. Tencent also has its own currency, called Q-coin. Unlike Facebook Credits, however, from early on Tencent members have used Q-coins outside the platform. While this was not an intended feature, Tencent had not taken measures against such use until prompted by state regulators.

Although it is a social network, in many respects Tencent resembles a freemium game, where players can participate for free but can buy a better experience if they spend money on the platform. When users open a profile, they start earning Q-coins in proportion to their activities. These Q-coins are provided by the platform itself. Users also earn a status that is linked to their "influence," which depends on the appearance of their page, activities, and connectedness. Users can also buy Q coins with state-issued currency—essentially buying status, which is again similar to freemium games. While it is only a small proportion of the members who buy Q-coins, those members are responsible for the vast majority of Tencent's revenues. Q-coins can then be used to play a large array of games on the platform. Indeed, Tencent is one of the largest gaming platforms in the world, itself developing many original games.

Tencent's Q-coin was introduced in the early 2000s. As mentioned earlier, Q-coins can be earned or bought. In theory, Q-coins are bound to each user's account and cannot be transferred directly. Nonetheless, there are ways to transfer them within the platform relatively easily.[15] Also, Q-coins cannot be—officially—exchanged back for state-issued currency.

Within a few years of its introduction, Q-coin gained significant traction outside of Tencent's own platform. Originally only intended for purchases of virtual goods and services, Q-coins became popular for peer-to-peer payments. Initially, people used Q-coins between close friends for simple transactions, say splitting a bill in a restaurant or sending "cash" gifts to each other, a popular Chinese custom. Gradually, online merchants started to accept Q-coins as payment. Some brick-and-mortar merchants followed as well. It was reported that you could buy groceries or get a haircut and pay with Q-coins using your Tencent account.[16]

The Chinese central bank, the People's Bank of China, started expressing its concerns about Q-coin's impact on the yuan in 2006, and those concerns grew stronger as the value of trade using Q-coins was increasing.[17] Tencent managers pointed to the restrictions on the currency's functionality as important mitigating factors. In February 2007, the Shanghai Daily reported Song Yang, an assistant public relations manager at Tencent, saying: "The fact that the Q-coins cannot be officially changed back into money makes them less than harmful to the financial market."[18]

However, as we mentioned before, full functionality is not necessary for a digital currency to have impact outside of its intended platform. Instead, a necessary—although not a sufficient—condition is transferability. With transferability, users can indirectly redeem Q-coins by transferring them among themselves inside the platform and exchanging state-issued currency outside the platform. As we saw, this was the case for the black markets for WoW gold. Furthermore, if the Q-coins are redeemable for goods and services, there may even be no need to exchange them for the state-issued currency.

Indeed, trade using Q-coins continued to increase and reportedly reached several billion renminbi by 2008. The following year, the Chinese government introduced regulation banning the exchange of a digital currency for real goods and services, in order to "limit its possible impact on the real financial system." Yet, today there is still a secondary market for Q-coins where people sell them for state-issued money. At the writing of this book, on Taobao, a trading platform, we saw a seller offering 50 Q-coins for 47.44 renminbi, whereas the "official rate" is 1 to 1. If one searches the term "buy Q-coin," over seven hundred thousand results appear—in other words, the market still seems pretty lively. While such transactions may not be as important today, there was a time when Q-coins filled a gap, acting as an easy to use payment system, essentially replacing credit cards. At the time when most Chinese did not have credit cards, e-commerce sites accepting Q-coins made trade somewhat easier.

With the prevalence of mobile platforms, Tencent's business developed two paths to mobile presence. On the one hand, Tencent has introduced a mobile app with a version of the well-known online platform, reoptimized for smartphones. In parallel, Tencent also introduced an entirely new social network built from scratch: WeChat. WeChat has evolved to become one of the most successful social networks today. Interestingly, Q-coins are not promoted on WeChat. In fact, they are not even usable there. WeChat uses state-issued currency and functions similarly to PayPal. It seems that the company wants WeChat to be an all-around e-commerce site where merchants can have a page and can promote and directly sell their products, similarly to Amazon or Alibaba.

3.2.4. Promotion Platforms and Amazon Coins

The last business model we analyze is promotion platforms. Promotion platforms are specialized two-sided platforms that bring together buyers and sellers. The role of the platform is to facilitate transactions between these groups of customers without really getting involved. Promotion platforms are somewhere between traditional stores and fully fledged markets such as the New York Stock Exchange or Amazon's e-commerce platform. The latter provide trading opportunities for a large and diverse set of stocks or products. In contrast, promotion platforms are markets with products that are closely linked. Game platforms, such as Valve's Steam, host a multitude of mostly similar games. These platforms often offer a proprietary currency to their users. One could think of these currency services as virtual wallets. The virtual currency can be purchased with state-issued currency but typically cannot be exchanged back to state-issued currency. Typically, it is not transferable, although one may be able to buy gifts for another user. In almost all cases, this relatively closed system serves some form of promotion activity.

To see this, let's consider a particular example: Amazon Coins. Customers get Amazon Coins when they buy

Amazon's Kindle Fire tablet. Otherwise, customers can only obtain Amazon Coins by purchasing them. Amazon Coins cannot be earned or transferred between customers. This last feature can sometimes create problems when, for example, Kindle Fire is purchased as a gift. Amazon Coins that come with the tablet cannot be later transferred to the recipient of the gift. The customers also cannot exchange Amazon Coins for state-issued currency. Finally, Amazon Coins can be spent only on a very limited selection of goods. It is often said that Amazon is the retailer with the largest selection on Earth, but Amazon Coins can only be spent on selected apps on Kindle Fire. To qualify, apps need to take advantage of the unique properties of Kindle Fire (as opposed to other tablets running on Android, for example).

Those properties are too restrictive for Amazon Coins to gain ground as a widely accepted currency. Why would Amazon not take advantage of its very large customer base and product selection by introducing an international currency—instead of restricting it so much? The answer is that the currency serves a particular promotional purpose. Amazon was a relative late comer to the tablets market. The market for tablets is another market characterized by network effects. However, this type of network effect is somewhat different from the one occurring among Facebook users. It is more similar to the network effect between Facebook users and Facebook app developers. We call these network effects *indirect*. The more applications that are available for a particular kind of a tablet, the more valuable the tablet is for the consumers, at least assuming that the quality of the apps on the competing platform are not significantly higher to compensate for the lower number of apps. In turn, developers want to develop applications for whichever tablet has the most consumers, as they will then have a larger base to whom the app could be sold. Thus, more apps attract more consumers, which attract more apps, which attract even more consumers. So, indirectly, the more popular the tablet is—that is, the more consumers have purchased it—the more attractive this tablet is to the next consumer, as it offers more apps. Hence we call them indirect network effects.

It is easy to see how this "large-grows-larger" dynamic gives rise to winner-take-all outcomes. Indirect network effects make it very hard to enter these markets. Usually successful entry into a market with network effects involves subsidizing or "bribing" one of the sides or the initial group of consumers to gain needed critical mass.[19] In the case of Amazon, lowering the price of Kindle Fire too much would hurt Amazon's revenue from this category. Instead, Amazon wanted to increase the value of the Kindle Fire tablet by having more apps available for users. However, just having more apps for Android would make all Android-based tablets more valuable. Amazon needed to procure apps that would be specific to Kindle Fire. One way would be to just pay developers for developing such apps. But that might be risky. If Amazon paid the developers upfront, how would they know whether the developers would develop really good apps that consumers would value? A solution is to give developers the money only after consumers "vote with their feet"—that is, purchase their apps. This way, the most valuable Kindle Fire–specific apps earn the most money, which gives developers incentive to develop better apps.

Customers who bought the second generation Kindle Fire for $199 got $50 in Amazon Coins. It may seem to be a rebate, but since the Coins can be spent only on the approved apps, it is not the same as lowering price. Customers cannot spend it freely. It could count as a rebate only for customers who wanted to spend $50 on Kindle Fire apps anyway, which is probably not the case for most customers. The developers know that for this particular platform, users have $50 on their hands that they can spend only on the apps. They will be more willing to spend Amazon Coins than regular cash, so they will be more likely to purchase approved apps. For the app to be approved for Amazon Coins payments, the app needs to demonstrate that it takes advantage of features specific to Kindle Fire, and thus that it increases the value of Kindle Fire more than it increases the value of other Android tablets. Just getting the app approved does not guarantee that its developers will get Amazon Coins. These apps are subject to ratings and reviews just as other apps. So, consumers will choose to purchase the most valuable of the approved apps. Amazon Coins that the developers collect can then be redeemed from Amazon, after the typical cut of 30 percent. Even though the developers can redeem Amazon Coins, the currency is still nonredeemable for the customers. Thus, Amazon is giving the $50 not to the customer purchasing Kindle Fire but to the developers who make Kindle Fire more valuable.

Easing any of the restrictions would be at odds with this goal. Allowing consumers to exchange Amazon Coins for state-issued currency would take away the incentive for the developers, because most people would take the cash or would spend the Coins on other items on Amazon.com that they wanted to purchase anyway. Accepting Amazon Coins in other areas of Amazon business would have the same effect. It would not help increase the network effects for Kindle Fire. And how about transferability? If Amazon Coins could be transferred between customers, this could result in a skewed distribution of Amazon Coins. Those few people who use a large number of Kindle Fire apps would get Amazon Coins from people who would rather spend this currency on other products. Those intensive app users would have lots of Amazon Coins, but they would not buy multiple copies of the same app. This would result in a larger number of distinctive apps purchased with Amazon Coins, but fewer copies per app. The best apps could see their market share shrinking, while some not so great apps would still be bought by the intensive app users. This would make the whole scheme less attractive for developers of the best apps. And, most important, it would not provide such strong incentives to produce the best apps. Thus, again, we see that Amazon Coins is a currency optimally designed for the purpose it is supposed to serve.

Steam Wallet Dollars

Video game platforms are another type of promotion platform. These platforms offer a collection of video games bringing together players and game developers. For players, they provide a convenient storefront with search capabilities and a digital wallet that may help them allocate their rewards and funds across various games. For game developers, they provide an advertising and promotion platform and an opportunity to build loyalty with their customers. As with Amazon Coins, it makes sense for the platform to offer a currency that can be spent across games, keeping people within the gaming platform's ecosystem. While people might get bored with a particular game, the platform provides an opportunity for them to spend whatever they have on other games on the platform.

Steam is an example of such a platform. Originally, it was developed by Valve, an online game developer, to provide a site from which gamers could download the updated versions of previously released games. It quickly became clear that the site could also serve as a distribution platform for new games. Once Valve's gamers became regular visitors on Steam for their updates and purchases, the company realized that it could open the platform for other developers to allow them to sell and update their games. As an early mover, Steam benefited from indirect network effects—gamers liked Steam because it had the largest variety of games and, similarly, game developers were attracted to Steam because of all the gamers visiting it. By the early 2000s, Steam has become one of the leading online distribution platforms. Yet, no matter how large, such a distribution platform does not necessitate a virtual currency. What then led to the introduction of Steam Wallet?

The answer is user generated content in games. In many online games, users can create small modifications, digital equipment, or new rules within the game that may be shared with other users. Sims, for example, is one such game that gained much more popularity when sharing became possible. From a technical perspective, the Steam platform was already well suited to serve such sharing across users. Yet, it could do even better by providing an incentive for the development of user generated content via the facilitation of trade. Along the way, the platform can make additional revenue. Steam introduced a wallet that users can feed with their credit cards, or gift cards purchased at game shops. Players can search for and acquire a very large variety of user generated content across the games available on the platform. Popular modifications are rewarded by paying their creators—that is, by crediting their Steam Wallet. Steam keeps a portion of the transaction as revenue.

Steam Wallet dollars are not redeemable for state-issued currency. As with Amazon Coins, they need to be spent within the Steam ecosystem. As this ecosystem grows, Steam has a strong incentive to keep its members spending money on the platform.

3.3. THE FUTURE OF PLATFORM-BASED CURRENCIES

The examples above illustrate how different attributes of currencies induce different usage and behavior of users. Therefore, the optimal set of attributes depends on the platform's business model.

A general design feature of platform-based currencies is not to allow for cash-out. This is directly related to the platforms' effort to increase loyalty and lock-in for their members. This is particularly important for platform businesses because there are strong consumption externalities leading to network effects. A member who keeps spending time on the platform will make the platform all the more attractive to others. This largely explains why most platform-based currencies have no cash-out options. A notable exception is the category of virtual worlds. As we saw, in this case, providing strong incentives for people to invest in the platform content requires the possibility for members to recoup their cash.

Strong network effects also favor the idea that users can buy the platform currency with state-issued currency. Again, this can only grow total activity on the platform and, in the presence of consumption externalities, make the platform more attractive to existing as well as new users. This argument has a limit in one particular case: when some platform-specific meritocracy is a key part of the platform's value proposition. Allowing for buying in may disturb this meritocracy and have a negative externality on the users. Indeed, if some sort of in-game meritocracy is important for the functioning of the platform then the platform should refrain from allowing buy-in for their members. This was most visible for the case of MMORPGs, where skill was important for all players to enjoy the game, and one could fake skills by purchasing certain items. Moreover, as we have seen, a dual currency system allows meritocracy to successfully coexist with economic exchange.

Transferability is probably the most critical design feature of a currency and the most nuanced. In practice, it is the only feature that is necessary, but not sufficient, for the currency to have impact outside of the platform. Transferability is necessary if the platform needs to promote economic activities for its value proposition, which is the case for many of the interactive business models. Yet, once transferability is allowed, it opens a back door for users to buy in and cash out even if the platform's policy aims to avoid that.

Are Restricted Currencies Really Currencies?

Most platform-based digital currencies are restricted in at least some of their attributes. Some, like Facebook Credits and Amazon Coins, are even restricted in transferability, arguably the most important attribute of a currency. One can legitimately ask whether restricted currencies are still money.

In the previous chapter, we discussed the economic definition of money and its limitations. Money is defined as a (1) unit of account, (2) store of value, and (3) medium of exchange. So are Facebook Credits, Amazon Coins, or WoW gold money? Some argue they are not. They have their own unit of account, even if they are pegged to a state-issued currency, but they are poor store of value, and one can hardly use them as a widely accepted medium of exchange in transactions.

However, WoW gold is definitely a currency—it is the currency of the World of Warcraft realm. You cannot use US dollars in World of Warcraft. The issue with Facebook Credits and Amazon Coins is more complicated. Their transfer and therefore role as a medium of exchange is limited. Facebook Credits can only be paid to Facebook. But then again, one could purchase Facebook items only with Facebook Credits, so Facebook Credit is a medium of exchange for such particular transaction. At the end of the day, currency should facilitate trade. One could argue that WoW gold or Amazon Coins can be used only for specific trades. But in some sense so does the US dollar and the Swedish krona. A currency may facilitate trade in a specific geographical area or only for a specific kind of trade. The more limited the trade it can facilitate, the more limited the currency. Traditionally, very limited currencies would not be viable. Nowadays, however, the design possibilities associated with digital currencies allow the creation of tailored currencies that are optimized for their narrow use.

Will Platform-Based Currencies Converge to a Single Currency?

Platform-based digital currencies are mostly limited to the use in a given platform. There is no reason to expect convergence toward one currency across platforms, as network effects are usually limited to one platform, and there are rarely network effects across platforms.

Moreover, using the same currency for multiple platforms requires a fair degree of coordination. This is possible when those platforms belong to the same family, say, different Zynga games, or if the use of currency is coordinated, as on the Steam platform or as attempted by Facebook with Facebook Credits. However, in most cases there will be one distinct currency on each platform that finds it beneficial to have a private currency. In some special cases, one platform may have more than one, as we saw with Guild Wars 2 or World of Warcraft after the adoption of the dual system. This can happen only if each of those currencies serves a different purpose. In the case of these MMORPGs, the multiplicity comes from the need to separate skill signaling from in-game economic activity.

CHAPTER 4

CRYPTOCURRENCIES

So far in this book, we saw digital currencies issued by digital platforms. These innovations are a good object to start with when analyzing the economics of digital currencies. However, when people hear "digital currency," their first thoughts will likely be "cryptocurrencies" and "Bitcoin." This is not surprising: for the past few years, these terms have appeared frequently in popular media, in technical discussions, and even in policy debates and legislation. We now move on to this second type of digital currencies, specify the main differences with platform-based digital currencies, and discuss what implications such differences have for the economics of cryptocurrencies and for their potential widespread adoption.

Before we do this, however, we would be remiss not to discuss the trigger (or, if you prefer, the culprit) of the ongoing media commotion: the Bitcoin. As we will see, Bitcoin is a decentralized digital currency invented in 2008 by somebody hiding behind the pseudonym of Satoshi Nakamoto. Nakamoto proposed Bitcoin to address an economic problem inherent in electronic commerce: the frictions and the high transaction costs of trading over the

Internet, particularly relevant for small-value transactions. Indeed, while the key innovation in Nakamoto's paper is cryptography and computer science, those who read it often comment on how much space it devotes to economics and a theory of money of the sort we discussed in the first chapters of this book.

In its early years, Bitcoin has been known to a relatively narrow community of cryptography enthusiasts. The first time the currency made it into the mainstream media was probably in June 2011, during the WikiLeaks affair. WikiLeaks is a website that publishes information, especially news leaks and secret information from classified sources. In 2010, WikiLeaks published a number of classified documents related to the war in Afghanistan, which brought mainstream media attention to the site and put WikiLeaks at odds with the US government. In December 2010, a number of banks and payment services providers (e.g., Bank of America, PayPal, and Visa) refused to provide WikiLeaks with their services, making it difficult if not impossible for the website to receive donations from its supporters. WikiLeaks' founder, Julian Assange, decided in June 2011 to start accepting donations in Bitcoin, highlighting the flexibility of the currency, its anonymity, and its independence from traditional financial providers.

Bitcoin grabbed the headlines again, in an even more spectacular manner, in late 2013, when it appeared to be an increasingly interesting speculative investment opportunity. Its price (i.e., its exchange rate to the US dollar) skyrocketed from below $15 at the beginning of 2013 to over $1,200 at the end of November 2013. At the same time, Bitcoin was gaining a foothold in electronic commerce. For example, Baidu, a Chinese search engine and the world's fifth most visited site, decided in October 2013 to start accepting Bitcoin for Jiasule, its commercial service for improving the security and performance of websites.

At the same time, another big reason for Bitcoin's presence in the media was its notoriety. The currency was at the center of several events and scandals. The biggest of them was the Silk Road raid by the Federal Bureau of Investigation (FBI). Silk Road was a website that matched buyers and sellers of illegal substances and services, for example drugs. The FBI estimated the revenue from the trades on Silk Road over the 2.5 years of the site's operation to be on the order of $1.2 billion. Bitcoin became the currency of choice for the parties to these illicit transactions, attracting them with its perceived anonymity and operations outside of the legal system. On October 2, 2013, US law enforcement shut down Silk Road and arrested Ross William Ulbricht, who in 2015 was convicted of running the site. In the process, the FBI seized about 26,000 bitcoins, then worth approximately $3.5 million.

All these events inevitably attracted regulators' and policymakers' attention to Bitcoin. In the United States, Senate hearings were held on Bitcoin on November 18–19, 2013. The digital currency made a generally positive impression, and even though policymakers stressed its potential risks, no immediate regulation was recommended. In some other countries, the reaction was harsher. China's central bank, likely still remembering the Q-coin episode we described in the previous chapter, banned financial institutions from handling the digital currency. Consequently, the Baidu website stopped accepting Bitcoin in December. Similarly, Vietnam's financial authorities made the currency outright illegal in that country.

In the presence of these and similar stories, Bitcoin made it to the mainstream news. Even though it lacked details, the general public heard about this "Bitcoin"—an emerging digital currency, with no central bank, defying national borders, which was gaining in value and popularity. Bitcoin has been touted as an instantaneous, anonymous, and free way to make transactions. It was starting to be perceived as a quicker and cheaper alternative to existing money, to be used in peer-to-peer transactions, international transfers, and so on. As we will see, at least some of this enthusiasm was misplaced. It turns out that paying with Bitcoin is not completely anonymous, and it is not always free or instantaneous. Nonetheless, Bitcoin is an ingenious development in computer science. Its major contribution that goes beyond its potential use as a currency is that it solves the double-spending problem in a decentralized network.

4.1. THE DOUBLE-SPENDING PROBLEM

The double-spending problem was the major stumbling block; for a long time, it was perceived to be an unsurmountable obstacle in the development of decentralized digital currencies. To illustrate its nature, we will begin with a simple thought experiment.

Suppose you had a technology that would allow you to perfectly copy money, say an ingenious photocopying machine that could quickly and easily duplicate banknotes. In Chapter 2, we mentioned counterfeiting traditional money—here we are talking about creating copies that would be absolutely indistinguishable from the originals.

If you were the only person with access to such technology, you might enjoy it for a while (we note that using it would, of course, be illegal—which is why we're keeping this discussion limited to a *thought* experiment). If instead this copying technology were widespread, nobody would care to work to earn money. Why bother with a job if you could simply copy the money you need? As long as you have a unit of money to start with, you can double and triple your money and so on, simply by copying it and multiplying the original as much as you wish. At the same time, nobody would want to sell anything to another person—why part with an object or a service if what you are getting in return is something you could have replicated yourself in the first place?

In other words, money would cease to function, and the economy would grind to a halt, unless it switched to a different, more difficult to copy, currency. This simple example illustrates that something that is easy to copy would not make very good money.

All this brings us to digital currency. Digital currency is essentially a string of zeros and ones, perhaps encoded on a magnetic strip, on a chip, or stored somewhere in the cloud. Regardless of where it sits, this piece of data is imminently copyable. We can reproduce it exactly, in as many copies as we wish, without harming the original. If money were simply electronic impulses, it seems we would be perilously close to the thought experiment above.

For a digital currency to serve as money, it needs to solve this problem of double spending. Perhaps the easiest solution is to keep a ledger, an account that would list each unit of the digital currency (perhaps by its serial number) and keep track who owns that unit at any given time. After a transaction, the ledger would be updated by changing the ownership of the currency unit from the buyer to the seller.

Keeping such a ledger is a good idea, but we have not yet solved the problem completely. After all, a ledger in the digital world is just a piece of data, and one can copy it as easily as before. For example, a dishonest buyer may copy the ledger prior to a transaction. While the ledger would be updated in any transaction, the dishonest buyer would try to revert to its prior version that still lists him as the owner of a unit of currency he has just spent. So, it seems we have merely replaced the problem of copying the digital currency with the problem of maintaining the integrity of the ledger.

Things would be different if we could designate a trusted third party that would be in charge of the ledger. The digital currency would then be centralized in a sense that the trusted party would be the only entity with the right to alter the ledger, and the third party would diligently and truthfully record all transactions in the ledger. All transactions would need to be reported to that trusted party, and sellers would consult it to verify that a prospective buyer has enough funds to complete a transaction.

Digital currencies managed in such a centralized fashion would and in fact do work. This is what banks do when they keep our deposit accounts or credit card accounts. All platform-based currencies we discussed in the previous chapter are also organized this way. Whether we talk about Amazon Coins or Facebook Credits, there is always an institution in the background that keeps track of all accounts and that stands ready to update the records whenever a transaction occurs. This institution has information about everybody's holdings and about all transactions that take place. This is very different from the anonymity of cash transactions.

Is it possible to design a decentralized digital currency—one that could operate as money with no centralized entity to keep track of the transactions? Initially, the consensus among computer scientists was that this would be difficult or perhaps just impossible—in fact, the e-cash problem was a long-standing challenge in computer science since the early 1980s. The solution to this puzzle was finally proposed in 2008 in a paper published by Satoshi Nakamoto, "Bitcoin: A Peer-to-peer Electronic Cash System." The impact of Nakamoto's paper has been immense. The solution he (or she, or they—we do not know who is behind the pseudonym) proposed, known as the Bitcoin protocol, was the first well-working solution to the problem of decentralized digital currency. More precisely, it was the first fully functional decentralized solution to the problem of double spending discussed above. As such, it is an important contribution to cryptography and to computer science in general. Moreover, as we will see later in this chapter, multiple hundreds of decentralized digital currencies have been proposed. While they differ on a number of dimensions, many of them share the reliance on the same general technology as Bitcoin does. All these currencies, including Bitcoin, are commonly referred to as cryptocurrencies, to reflect the idea that the soundness of the system depends only on the algorithm and cryptographic tools it uses.

4.2. HOW DOES BITCOIN WORK? BRIEF OVERVIEW

We will limit our discussion of how Bitcoin works to a high-level overview that avoids some of the technical intricacies and the computer-scientific innovation the Bitcoin is justly famous for.[1] Our intention is not to give a detailed description of the inner workings of Bitcoin but rather to illustrate the mechanism and, especially, the incentives the mechanism provides for the system to work. We will try to be technical only insomuch as it contributes to a better appreciation of the economic forces affecting the currency.

Most important, as we signaled above, all transactions involving bitcoins are written in a public ledger. That ledger is available to anyone and is transparent—at any given time, you can trace the path of all transactions a given bitcoin (or part of a bitcoin) has been involved in. At the same time, the parties in the transactions are identified not by name but by a string of letters and numbers. The ledger is updated by the overall Bitcoin community—it is the "public" that writes the transactions in the ledger and with that validates them. This community is commonly referred to as the Bitcoin network, or Bitcoin system, with capital "B." The lowercase "bitcoin" is used for the currency units, also abbreviated BTC. The spelling convention, however, is sometimes different for other cryptocurrencies.

When a transaction is made, the ledger is appended with the information on the number of coins moved and the Bitcoin address to which they are moved. The address is a string of 26 to 35 alphanumeric characters and is intended to be shared. This is why it is often referred to as "public" Bitcoin address. When a person wants to pay with bitcoins, the transaction is broadcasted to the network, along with a signature, based on the sender's private key and the receiver's address.[2] The private key is also a string of alphanumeric characters of varying length. Because it is mathematically related to the address the bitcoin was last sent to, it proves that the sender has the right to spend this bitcoin. All this means that the proposed transaction has embedded information about past transactions. Since the sender's key is the only thing that is needed to create a valid signature, aside from the receiver's address, owners of bitcoins are well advised to keep their private key secret. Otherwise, anyone who knows the private key can send the bitcoins related to the key to the address he or she controls. This system is called public-key cryptography and is commonly applied in many Internet systems, like email or login passwords.

The procedure of broadcasting transactions is actually broadly similar to what happens in a centralized network, say when one pays with Q-coins or Amazon Coins or pays from a bank account. There too you need to prove that you have the right to spend a given coin, although you do this in a different manner. When dealing with platform-based currencies or a bank, you identify yourself by logging into the platform, which keeps track of all holdings of digital currency in your account. When you transact with somebody, the platform checks that the funds are indeed available in the account and adjusts the balance of your account and the account you are transacting with. It also issues a confirmation that the funds were transferred.

The key innovation in Bitcoin is that such a trusted third party is no longer necessary. First of all, the ledger is publically available in the form called the *blockchain*. The blockchain is simply the record of all Bitcoin transactions ever completed. That includes records of the minting of new bitcoins and the party that was allocated this newly issued bit of the currency. When that person spends their bitcoins, the new transaction is sent to the Bitcoin network to be appended at the end of the blockchain, allowing everybody to track the movement of bitcoins from one address to another.

Importantly, sending this information does not yet conclude the transaction. In a very direct sense, the hard work only begins at that stage. New transactions are collected into a block that needs to be added to the blockchain.

The transactions are verified by checking against the blockchain that the bitcoins are sent by someone who has received them earlier and that they have not been spent before. This verification is computationally easy. However, for the addition to the blockchain to be recognized, a Bitcoin network participant must complete *proof-of-work*, which is to solve a complicated and very computationally intense puzzle posted by the system.[3] Network participants who approach this challenge are called miners. The puzzle is solved by brute calculation force—that is, by trial and error. Therefore, the more computing power you have, the quicker you can propose and check potential answers, and the faster you can expect to find a solution. The puzzle is a one-way puzzle, based on a hashing function algorithm. "One-way" means that while a valid solution to the problem is difficult to find, it is quick and easy to verify by others in the Bitcoin network.

The main role of the proof-of-work is to ensure immutability of the ledger. The solution to the puzzle becomes a part of the block being added to the blockchain. Importantly, the solution depends on the blocks preceding it in the blockchain. Suppose you wanted to go back and change a transaction, for example replacing the recipient of the bitcoins being sent with yourself. This would change one of the past blocks, meaning you would need to redo the proof-of-work for that block to make it a valid addition to the blockchain. Even more important, you would also need to redo the proof-of-work for all the blocks that follow it. You would need 51 percent of the computing power of the whole network to outperform other miners in order to successfully put fraudulent blocks into the blockchain. Gaining such computational power is very costly, which was the intent in Bitcoin network design.

The proof-of-work also formalizes the incentives for miners to participate in the Bitcoin network, keep their machines running, and help ensure that new transactions are being processed. Participation is costly, and the system needs to promise a reward, or at least a possibility of a reward, for people to do that. Proof-of-work is a way to formalize that promise.

The first miner to arrive at a valid solution gets to attach the block to the blockchain and receives a batch of newly minted bitcoins as reward. The appended block-chain is then sent to the rest of the Bitcoin network. All miners also working on this transaction (more precisely, on a block of transactions including the current one) lose the race, accept the block, and need to move on to other transactions. The puzzle depends on both the block of transactions being added and the overall blockchain, so any miners working on different transactions and using an older version of the blockchain also need to restart their work.

This creates a tournament structure for the miners. They compete one against another (sometimes, individual miners merge their computing power to compete as a mining pool), and the reward they earn is all or nothing: either they are the first to solve the puzzle and get the reward or their investment in the puzzle is lost. Initially, bitcoins were mined on regular computers.[4] But nowadays, the investment in solving the puzzle is not inconsequential. Becoming a meaningful miner in the Bitcoin network requires a fixed investment in the hardware, for example, application specific integrated circuit (ASIC) machines designed to focus on solving a particular problem, in this case, a Bitcoin puzzle. It also requires time during which that computing power could be spent on something else, and considerable amounts of electricity. That last element is important enough for serious miners to locate in places where the cost of electricity and of cooling their machines is low, for example, in Iceland. [5]

The Bitcoin algorithm allows for a block to be added to the blockchain about every 10 minutes. This pace is ensured by automatically adjusting the difficulty of the "puzzle" so that it takes about 10 minutes for the network to solve it. And thus every 10 minutes a miner gets new coins. The number of coins awarded for adding a block, initially set at 50 bitcoins, is halved every 210,000 blocks, so approximately every 4 years. Since November 28, 2013, adding a new block rewards 25 bitcoins. Eventually this halving process will result in only one satoshi (0.00000001 of bitcoin) as the miner's reward, and after four years, approximately in 2140, there will be no reward. By then, the total amount of all minted bitcoins will be fixed at just under 21 million. This design decision was motivated by the desire to assure scarcity of bitcoins—in a way to make them similar to gold. But, as we will see later, this may have deflationary consequences for the Bitcoin economy.

Once Bitcoin reaches its fixed supply, there will be no new bitcoins to provide the incentive to participate. Instead, miners will be compensated with fees paid by the parties to each transaction. Interestingly, the Bitcoin algorithm allows for fees even today, and many transactions involve such fees already. Fees are voluntarily added by the sender of bitcoins. The fee is collected by the miner who adds this particular transaction to the blockchain. Therefore, adding fees increases the probability that the transaction will be verified and added to the blockchain sooner, as the miners pay attention to include fee-paying transactions in their blocks. At present, fees are relatively small (on the order of 0.0001 of bitcoin), with the main reward for mining being the newly issued bitcoins. One could imagine that in the future such fees will be set by competitive forces: the supply of the computing power on the side of miners and the demand for transaction verification on the side of the bitcoin buyers and sellers.

The key technical innovation, the absence of a centralized trusted third party, makes Bitcoin very different from platform-based currencies and has important implications for the economics of the currency. At the same time, Bitcoin is, on many dimensions, more similar to centralized digital currencies than most people expect.

For example, Bitcoin is often thought to be the digital equivalent of cash: anonymous and hardly possible to trace once spent. This is at best a simplification. The blockchain is an exact record of the path of all the addresses a bitcoin was sent to, which means that Bitcoin is more correctly described as a "pseudonymous" currency than as an "anonymous" currency. Moreover, the record of all prior transactions is stored in the ledger openly and is transparent to all Bitcoin users. In practice, few users would be determined enough, or would have enough resources, to be able to track the transactions and the bitcoin holdings directly to the real-life people involved. This makes the currency sufficiently opaque and sufficiently anonymous for some nefarious purposes. Nonetheless, institutions with ample resources can track the movement of bitcoins closely enough to be able to identify the real-life identity of the users of currency. For example, when the FBI has investigated the Silk Road website described above, they were able to identify the person responsible for the website and track funds flowing into his account.

Similarly, a bitcoin is sometimes thought to be easy to lose. However, this is at least conceptually similar to centralized, or platform-based, currencies. You can lose your bitcoins if you lose your private key, the piece of data that identifies you as the party owning the bitcoins. This is similar to losing your password to a website that issued you a platform-based currency. You might be able to regain your access and your holdings if you can prove to the platform that you are who you say you are, perhaps by answering a secret question or proving that you have access to the email account associated with this account. If you cannot prove who you are, you will not be able to retrieve your holdings, and they will be lost to you. In the Bitcoin network, the only way you can identify yourself is by providing your private key.[6]

Moreover, suppose your bitcoin holdings are hacked (perhaps because you used an electronic wallet, a piece of software responsible for managing your bitcoin, from a dubious source). If the hacker spends your bitcoins, you have little hope of regaining them. In principle, you could be in similar trouble if somebody steals the password to your account on a digital-currency issuing platform. That person would have the power to spend the currency, although the spending could be limited to articles less attractive for them, such as apps that can only be loaded to your own account. A difference specific to platform-based and other centralized currencies is that the issuer may in principle stand ready to reverse fraudulent or erroneous transactions and undo the damage the attack may have caused.

Finally, people often claim that Bitcoin is a costless way to transact. This is a misperception. As we saw, many transactions even today involve fees, although such fees are currently very small. Moreover, the cost of mining—the equipment and electricity—is very large.[7] This cost is at present diffused across the overall Bitcoin network and hence may seem invisible to many participants. Arguably, this is similar to a platform-based digital currency that seems free to use, even though it is costly for the platform to maintain the infrastructure required to do so.

4.3. NOT THE FIRST ONE— PREDECESSORS OF BITCOIN

Our description of how Bitcoin works is by intent simplified, so we can focus on economic forces and competition later in this chapter. But even from this simplified description, one can see that it is very demanding to construct a decentralized currency system that solves the double-spending problem. In fact, it took many attempts to do so. Bitcoin was not the first decentralized digital currency. However, it was the first one that worked well enough to gain some acceptance by the general public. And in its system, Bitcoin incorporated many of the earlier solutions. The cryptography community was interested in developing a decentralized currency system since the rise of the Internet.

The first piece of Bitcoin-like technology was *hashcash*, a system based on proof-of-work introduced in 1997 by Adam Beck. Beck's purpose was to prevent email spam by requiring the sender's computer to do computational work before sending the email. Such work would be relatively trivial for an individual email and would not affect computer performance. However, it would make sending thousands or millions of emails prohibitively costly in terms of computing power, making sending mass spam emails uneconomical. The ingenuity of hashcash is that it obtained this goal without charging money for emails. As we saw, Satoshi Nakamoto incorporated this element into Bitcoin to make it costly to create a fake blockchain.

In 1998, Wei Dai designed a decentralized digital currency, called *b-money* that would allow for anonymous peer-to-peer transactions. The transactions would be recorded by the members of the network in a ledger. Each participant would have a copy of the ledger. To fight misconduct—for example, to prevent participants from recording transactions that did not happen—the nodes in the system had to deposit money to a common pool. The deposited money was used for fines for misconduct and rewards for proof of misconduct. Such a system of fines and rewards, however, is difficult to enforce without a central authority to decide and solve disagreements.

In 2005, Nick Szabo proposed *bit-gold*, which also used proof-of-work and a distributed property title registry, similar to later Bitcoin's ledger. The work of solving a one-way puzzle was used to create new pieces of bit-gold, but there was no clear control over how much bit-gold can be created and how quickly. Szabo himself raised a concern that a powerful computer could "swamp the market with bit gold," lowering its value because the market will adjust.[8]

B-money and bit-gold were ideas, theoretical considerations, which were never really implemented, making it difficult to know how well they would work. They had never captured enough interest from people outside the small group of cryptography enthusiasts.

B-money, bit-gold, and, later, Bitcoin were developed by enthusiasts to satisfy the need for anonymity in digital transactions. There were also commercial efforts to create anonymous digital currency systems. Similar to Bitcoin, these systems comprised independent currency units, they allowed for greater divisibility, and they involved a universal permanent ledger of transactions. However, those systems were centralized. Two of the best-known examples are DigiCash and Citibank's e-cash called Electronic Monetary System.

DigiCash was a commercial company, set up in 1989 by David Chaum, and it proposed building a system of anonymous electronic cash to governments and banks. The DigiCash system had asymmetric anonymity: the payer was anonymous, whereas the payee could be "irrefutably identified if needed." This feature was motivated by the desire to end corruption and organized crime. The innovation of the system was the ability to transport information wirelessly, and thus it was well suited to pay road tolls, which was supposed to be its first use. David Chaum had even signed a contract with the Dutch government for this purpose. The idea of the DigiCash system also attracted some attention beyond toll application. There was interest from banks (such as Deutsche Bank and Credit Suisse), Visa, and Microsoft. By the end of 1990s, however, everything fell apart, including the company itself. For a few years, one bank in the United States, The Mark Twain Bank of St. Louis, Missouri, was using DigiCash. The initiative was, however, terminated in 1997.

The second example of commercial development of a decentralized digital currency was Citibank's e-cash. In the 1990s, Citibank was developing a system of electronic money in-house. The money had the interesting feature that it expired after some time, and the holder needed to contact the bank to replace it. This feature was meant to prevent money laundering. There were test runs and pilot programs in 1997 and 2001. In 2001, the project was shut down by the new management of Citigroup.[9]

Bitcoin took some elements of these earlier systems and combined them in a new innovation. That innovation had some elements that had been common and expected by then, for example its peer-to-peer nature (anyone with a computer could become part of the network) or its use of public-key encryption with private key. Its novelty and importance came from combining the idea of a blockchain—a public ledger that would be prohibitively costly to forge due to proof-of-work—and mining—the monetary incentive system to encourage the nodes to keep the ledger up to date. These two features allow users to keep the system honest while fighting off hackers.

4.4. NEW CHALLENGES

For all its ingenuity, Bitcoin is not without flaws. We have already seen one of them: the substantial and still increasing cost of mining new bitcoins. The most obvious part of the cost is the electricity. Moreover, one needs a substantial investment to be competitive in the mining business. It is no longer enough to own a cluster of computers, one needs specialized mining rigs designed to solve the proof-of-work puzzle as efficiently as possible.

We see an arms race in the mining business, with miners continually investing in new hardware to build a competitive edge and pushing their competitors to do the same. Initially, bitcoins were mined with regular computers. Eventually, one of the early miners noticed that one could take advantage of the graphics card to get a computational advantage in mining. This gave rise to designing devices that would be ever more efficient in solving the Bitcoin puzzle.

This ruthless race toward new and more powerful technology arises because of the tournament structure of the Bitcoin algorithm. Since the winner of the mining puzzle takes the whole reward, even slight improvements that put a miner just a bit ahead of everyone else give the miner a large expected reward. At any given point, the incremental investment may seem small and be worthwhile, but when in response everyone else also invests and catches up, the total investment of the overall mining industry may easily become worth more than the value that miners can win.

The race is sped up by a particular feature of the Bitcoin system: the difficulty of the cryptographic puzzles is adjusted to keep the expansion of the blockchain to a constant pace of one block being added every 10 minutes. The introduction of more powerful mining rigs effectively increases the difficulty of the puzzle. Since miners have more computing power at their disposal, they solve any given puzzle in a shorter time; to slow them down, the puzzle must be made more complex by requiring more cryptographic operations to be conducted. This in turns leads to increased energy use: even though new mining rigs are designed to operate more efficiently, running more computations typically requires more electricity.

An interesting consequence of Bitcoin's tournament structure is the appearance of mining pools. Mining pools are co-ops of miners who divide the mining tasks among themselves and share any rewards, typically proportionally to the computing power contributed to the pool. For individual miners, the incentive to get into the pool is to lower the uncertainty of going it alone. Winning the puzzle is profitable but very unlikely for an individual miner. Instead, participating in a pool allows users to share the risk and essentially insure one another. The pool wins more frequently than any individual does. Although, of course, it brings a lower reward when winning, as the newly mined bitcoins and fees earned need to be spread across the whole pool. For many miners, this tradeoff is attractive. They prefer to forego the possibility of large but infrequent prizes for the prospect of a steady accumulation of smaller rewards.

Overall, this type of mining leads to three broad categories of costs. First, there are the costs driven by the energy use by the specialized mining machines. Second, the system induces uneven participation in the network: elite miners, who invest in mining rigs, may end up controlling the ledger while collecting new bitcoins, which further allow them to afford updated mining machinery. Third, and as a consequence of the above, we may observe overinvestment in mining equipment.

At the time of writing, an important consequence of the rising energy costs is the externality it imposes on the environment and on the overall economy. This externality is amplified because many of the computations underlying Bitcoin end up being ultimately useless.[10] Because of the winner-take-all tournament structure, only the computations of the miner who wins the race are important in a sense of their result being incorporated into the blockchain. All other miners who were working at the same time lose the competition, and all computations they were working on need to be discarded—since the hashing problem is solved essentially through trial and error, those computations are not useful for any subsequent blocks the miners may be working on. From this point of view, the energy spent on the discarded computations is a loss to the system.

Nonetheless, so far the revenues from mined bitcoins offset the energy costs, and make mining economically viable for individual miners, at least those who invested in higher quality and efficiency mining equipment. However, this situation will eventually change. As we described earlier, the rate at which the Bitcoin algorithm generates new bitcoins is decreasing over time. It is unlikely that the price of bitcoin will increase at the same rate, which means that the reward for mining new coins will gradually go down. Eventually, the high energy costs will catch up with the declining profits. This alone is unlikely to shut down the system, but it will make fees crucial. At the moment, many Bitcoin transactions are conducted with minimal fees (a small fraction on a bitcoin, optional but usually imposed by the digital wallets people use) or even no fees. Eventually, these fees will need to increase to offset the drop in the new bitcoins created and in the energy costs, which are probably unlikely to drop at a similar rate.

Of the three drawbacks we discussed here, the rise of elite miners may become an even more serious challenge to Bitcoin because of its potential to lead to the "51 percent attack." The Bitcoin system maintains the integrity of the blockchain by relying on a diffuse network of miners who effectively keep each other honest. This system of distributed checks fails when a miner, or a coordinated group of miners, gains control over more than half of the computing power underlying the network. In such a case, the super-miner would be able to take control of the ledger, with powers ranging from preventing new transactions from being added to the blockchain to potentially engaging in double spending.

Mining arms race makes it more likely that such a super-miner appears.[11] First, the arms race forces less efficient miners, or miners who cannot afford improvements to their mining rig, out of the system. Even if those miners stay in the network, they will have a relatively lower share of the total computing power. With fewer high-power participants, it becomes more likely that one of them will dominate the network. Mining pools also increase the threat of 51 percent attack. As we explained above, the arms race gives miners incentives to pool their resources into mining pools. Such pools aggregate the computing power of individual miners, making it easier for the overall pool to exceed 50 percent of the network's computing power. One of the major innovations in Bitcoin was eliminating the need for a trusted third party who would monitor and manage the network. A miner or a mining pool that controls more than half of the network will essentially become such a third party dominating the network. Ironically, it would not even be clear if such an entity may or may not be a "trusted" third party.

The threat of a 51 percent attack is not purely academic. In mid-2014, it was reported[12] that Ghash.io, one of the largest Bitcoin mining pools, has briefly reached 50 percent of the computing power of the overall Bitcoin network. There was no damage to the system, because, as the pool explained, there was no nefarious intent.

Another weakness of Bitcoin is the potential deflationary pressure built into its algorithm. As we saw earlier, the supply of bitcoins—that is, the number of the bitcoins in existence—is increasing but is doing so at a decreasing pace, and at some stage, the supply will become fixed. This feature was consciously built into the design, but may have unintended consequences. The scarcity may translate into downward pressure on prices denominated in bitcoin—with fewer coins to go around, consumers may not want to spend too many coins on a given good.

Why would the limited supply of bitcoins translate into decreasing prices? To explain this phenomenon, we can use an economic theory called the "quantity theory of money."

The theory links four economic quantities: the supply of money, M; the velocity of money, V (that is, how quickly money circulates in the economy); the goods and services the economy produces, Y; and the price of these products, P. These quantities are linked through an identity,

$$MV = PY$$

That identity is widely accepted among economists (after all, it is an identity), and it has an appealing interpretation. The size of the economy (think GDP) is based on the number of goods and services that are being traded (Y) and on their prices (P). The sum total of these transactions needs to be supported by the money circulating in the economy. If money circulates very slowly (low velocity V), you need more of it to support the economy. For example, suppose that each unit of the currency, say, each separate dollar, can only be used once per year ($V=1$). This means that to support the GDP of $100 (the value of all goods and services equal to $100), we need 100 separate dollars (or combination of separate banknotes and coins that add up to $100).

The above identity helps us understand what happens when more goods are produced in the economy; that is, when Y increases. If the supply of money, M, is constant, and if the velocity of money, V, does not change, there is only one possibility: prices must drop. If they did not, we would not have enough money in the economy to support all the transactions that underlie the total production.

What does this theory predict for Bitcoin? First, note that as soon as the supply of bitcoins is fixed, the supply of money, M, will be constant, or even decline, as some of the bitcoins may be lost, if their owners misplace their private keys. If Bitcoin gains popularity and more people decide to use it, there will be more products offered and purchased in the Bitcoin economy; that is, Y will increase. The quantity theory of money tells us that in response, the level of prices, P, should drop proportionally. Simply put, there will not be enough bitcoins to support the increased spending, and in response, prices will need to adjust.

Of course, a drop in prices is not inevitable. It may be that the fourth term of our equation, the velocity of money, V, adjusts instead. If each bitcoin circulates in the economy faster than before, then the same supply of bitcoins will be able to support a larger volume of spending. It may not be clear how exactly Bitcoin velocity may increase, but it is a theoretical possibility. A perhaps less attractive outcome would be a cap on the growth of the Bitcoin economy. If Bitcoin's use is limited to a relatively stable volume of goods and services (i.e., when Y above is fixed), then prices may not change even though money supply is constant. Either way, the identity above tells us that something has to budge: it would be shortsighted to think that the size of the Bitcoin economy can change without having an impact on the level of prices.[13]

While falling prices may seem like a good thing, they tend to have an adverse effect on the economy. For example, people anticipating lower prices in the future will postpone their consumption and investments, which reduces the current size of the economy.

Given the above reasoning, why was it decided that the total supply of bitcoins would be constant? The likely reason was to build in an element of scarcity into the design of the cryptocurrency to ensure that it cannot be inflated. In the context of traditional currencies, inflation is often triggered by an increase in the supply of money.[14] The failsafe built into Bitcoin works so well, however, as to tilt the balance in the opposing direction and err on the side of deflation.

To offset the deflationary tendency, one may imagine introducing a gradual increase of the money supply into the Bitcoin algorithm. The problem then becomes getting the rate of increase exactly right, to ensure that prices remain relatively constant. It is doubtful (at best, debatable) whether there is a prespecified formula that could achieve this goal; instead, in most countries, similar adjustments are left to central banks. Judging from the narrative accompanying Bitcoin, at least some of its users are willing to accept the potential instability in prices in return for being independent of an institution such as a central bank. For such Bitcoin users, this feature in Bitcoin's design is perceived as positive, and it would contribute to Bitcoin's higher adoption by such users.

4.5. COMPETITION AGAINST OTHER CRYPTOCURRENCIES

We saw that the original Bitcoin algorithm has some unpleasant externalities (e.g., the high electricity usage) and drawbacks that may affect its economic viability (e.g., the deflationary pressure). Because the Bitcoin algorithm is publicly available and free for people to copy and improve on, a number of alternative cryptocurrencies—often referred to as "altcoins"—have appeared, fixing the real, and sometimes only perceived, weaknesses in the Bitcoin design. In many cases, these new cryptocurrencies work in a very similar manner as the original Bitcoin. Just as Bitcoin, they have no centralized authority (trusted third party) that would oversee the transactions and record them against users' accounts. Instead, these currencies rely on cryptography to maintain and distribute a ledger (blockchain) that reflects all transactions in a given currency. The ecology of such cryptocurrencies is also similar to that of Bitcoin. The participants in the system verify the proposed transactions; usually, a group of participants (miners) needs to solve complicated mathematical "puzzles" to enter the new transactions into the ledger.

Creating a new altcoin is a business with relatively low barriers to entry. As Bitcoin attracted attention outside of the cryptography community in the late 2013, the number of cryptocurrencies based on Bitcoin's protocol skyrocketed. Some of these new cryptocurrencies are little more than a copy of Bitcoin (for example, Terracoin). Others differ in a technical detail; for example, Litecoin uses a different hashing algorithm than Bitcoin does but is otherwise very similar. Yet others propose a more extensive change to the algorithm, with the potential to meaningfully change the economic forces behind the cryptocurrency.

We now overview some of the altcoins, focusing on the ones that gained more popularity or those that improved on the Bitcoin's weaknesses that we discussed earlier in this chapter. We will then discuss the consequences of the competition across these various cryptocurrencies. Table 4.1 summarizes a few of these cryptocurrencies and describes the main design choices they adopted.

Litecoin
One of the first altcoins that followed Bitcoin was Litecoin. Litecoin was created in October 2011 by Charles Lee. The main driving force behind its introduction was frustration with the complexity of the cryptographic tools used in Bitcoin, particularly the hashing algorithm Bitcoin uses, SHA-256. The algorithm imposes substantial computational burden on Bitcoin miners and forces them to invest heavily in their hardware if they want to remain competitive. Consequently, Bitcoin miners who were able to upgrade to using video cards and ASIC equipment—at

Table 4.1 Summary of attributes of selected cryptocurrencies

Cryptocurrency	Algorithm	Money supply	Other attributes
Bitcoin	proof-of-work SHA-256	fixed amount of coins	
Litecoin	proof-of-work scrypt	larger, but fixed amount	
Feathercoin	proof-of-work NeoScrypt	even larger, but fixed amount	
Peercoin	proof-of-work SHA-256 + proof-of-stake	unlimited (after reaching certain level, annual 1 percent increase in supply)	
Novacoin	proof-of-work scrypt + proof-of-stake	unlimited (after reaching certain level, annual 1 percent increase in supply)	
Darkcoin	proof-of-work initially SHA-256, later changed to X11	fixed amount	more anonymity (by coin mixing)
Cloakcoin	proof-of-stake anonymity	fixed amount	more anonymity (by unique stealth addresses)
Dogecoin	proof-of-work scrypt	unlimited (after reaching certain level, 10,000 per block indefinitely— about 5.256 billion per year)	intended for tipping (transfer of small amounts)

(*Continued*)

Table 4.1   (Continued)

Cryptocurrency	Algorithm	Money supply	Other attributes
Karmacoin	initially proof-of-work scrypt; now proof-of-work X11 + proof-of-stake	fixed amount	intended for tipping
Reddcoin	initially proof-of-work scrypt; now proof-of-stake velocity	fixed amount	intended for tipping

the time, state of the art hardware for mining Bitcoin—dominated the mining business.

Litecoin set out to solve the problem of excessive energy use and the "arms race" among the miners. To do so, Litecoin proposed to use a different hashing algorithm for the proof-of-work than Bitcoin does—*scrypt* instead of SHA-256. Scrypt requires relatively less computing power, lowering the amount of electrical energy that mining needs and making it possible to mine litecoins using standard PCs at a time when mining bitcoins successfully already required specialized equipment.

Solving this problem is important for a number of reasons. First, it is certainly worthwhile to try to economize on the use of electrical energy required to solve the cryptographic puzzle underlying a given cryptocurrency algorithm. People who use the cryptocurrency care about this not only because they are environmentally conscious (although some of them undoubtedly are). There is also a more prosaic reason: the costs of running a cryptocurrency are in essence born by everybody who uses that cryptocurrency. If the costs are too high (e.g., higher than the expected reward earned by miners), the currency will not be sustainable in the first place; and would be even less likely to become a potential challenger to other cryptocurrencies or to state-issued currencies. We will come back to these issues later in this chapter.

The second reason why it was important to slow down, or even stop, the arms race between the miners is the risk of mining becoming concentrated across the very few players who are able to afford the largest and the fastest mining rigs. The issue here is the "51 percent attack" that we described earlier. As miners try to outbid one another to keep up in the arms race, the miners with fewer resources may be quickly left behind, and they may decide to drop out of the mining pool. With fewer participants, the importance of those miners who continually invest in the best technology will increase, making it likely that one of them, or an organized group of such miners acting together, will eventually have more than half of the computing power in the cryptocurrency system. Such a group may or may not be benevolent toward the rest of the cryptocurrency ecosystem, but it opens up a risk that the system collapses.

All of this means that the Litecoin's innovation was well meant and was aimed at addressing an important risk in the Bitcoin's design. However, the way that Litecoin approached this issue has not changed the incentives of the participants in the cryptocurrency ecosystem and has ultimately failed to resolve the arms race problem in mining. The underlying algorithm still has the tournament structure that rewards the miner with the most powerful machine, at least on average. This means that as Litecoin became more popular, miners had an increasingly stronger incentive to invest in more powerful machines to make it more likely that they would outcompete other miners.

The algorithm itself magnified this effect: as faster computers appeared, the Litecoin network increased the difficulty of the mining task, which by itself pushed miners to upgrade their equipment.

The ASIC equipment that had been developed for Bitcoin was specialized for the SHA-256 hashing function and could not be adapted for Litecoin's scrypt. However, as Litecoin became more popular, demand grew for mining rigs customized for scrypt. It eventually became economical for ASIC manufacturers to design equipment specialized for scrypt. Nowadays, it is virtually impossible to mine Litecoin with a PC, because it is primarily mined by ASIC miners. This has led to the very situation that Charles Lee tried to avoid when designing Litecoin.

The second main difference between Bitcoin and Litecoin is in the total supply of the coins. While the supply of bitcoins is limited to 21 million, there will be many more litecoins created—84 million in total. This change was proposed to address a concern commonly raised for Bitcoin: the potential for deflation caused by the fixed supply of the currency. Unfortunately, increasing the total number of coins four times relative to Bitcoin does little to change the deflationary incentives. This is because Litecoin users are aware that the supply is finite and that it will stop growing at a known date. This leads to the same problem as the one we described for Bitcoin: the finite number of coins is increasingly ineffective in servicing a potentially growing number of transactions, making coins relatively scarcer and hence more valuable. Consequently, prices drop—over time, it will take fewer litecoins to buy a given good or service. Quadrupling the number of coins changes the esthetics of the problem but does not solve it. Perhaps the easiest way to see that is to imagine that people's holdings of a currency suddenly multiply by four. The most obvious consequence of this "devaluation" would be that all prices would quadruple as well, making everybody exactly as wealthy, or as poor, as they were before.

Finally, another meaningful attempt to improve Litecoin in comparison to Bitcoin was to allow for a quicker validation of transactions. While Bitcoin processes each block of transactions every 10 minutes, Litecoin is designed to process a block four times faster, every 2.5 minutes. This feature indeed makes a difference— Litecoin is quicker to validate transactions than Bitcoin is. We would, however, argue that this improvement does relatively little to alter incentives in the Litecoin ecosystem.[15]

Overall, while Litecoin recognized a number of important flaws in the design of Bitcoin, the way it set out to avoid those flaws was not necessarily successful.

Feathercoin

Another attempted improvement on the design of Bitcoin, and that of Litecoin, was Feathercoin, a cryptocurrency introduced by Peter Bushnell in April 2013. It has a very similar design to Litecoin. For example, just as Litecoin specifies that the total supply of coins will be four times the limit of Bitcoin, Feathercoin aims to have a total circulation four times larger than Litecoin's is. Unfortunately, as we saw, this is not a good way to undo the deflationary incentives inherent in the design of the currency.

A larger difference and arguably an improvement in the design of Feathercoin is the hashing algorithm used for the proof-of-work. Feathercoin uses the newly developed NeoScrypt, a version of scrypt that was especially modified to protect against ASIC-style mining rigs. This change aims at "democratizing" mining and saving overall energy

costs associated with the cryptocurrency. The desired consequence is to attract miners who cannot afford to successfully mine in ASIC-dominated environments, which, by
2013, included both Bitcoin and Litecoin. Nonetheless,
even at the introduction of NeoScrypt, it was admitted
that it would not solve the problem of ASIC completely; it
might merely postpone it into the future. This should not
be too surprising. Any proof-of-work algorithm will favor
higher computational power and will give an advantage
to whomever wields such power, no matter how small the
difference between that miner and the next-most powerful miner. This gives miners incentives to engage in an
arms race, which in turn may give an incentive for hardware producers to develop mining rigs specialized for
NeoScrypt as soon as they see enough demand. In other
words, we ended up with the dynamics familiar to us from
both Bitcoin and Litecoin. It is possible of course that at
this stage a brand new cryptocurrency may be proposed
with a slightly different hashing algorithm, which will
allow miners to remain a step ahead of hardware designers.
Clearly, however, this is merely postponing the undesired
outcome, not eliminating it completely.

Peercoin

As we saw, the problems of the arms race and of excessive energy consumption arise because of the tournament
nature of the proof-of-work system in the early cryptocurrencies. Once it became clear that neither Litecoin nor
Feathercoin could solve this issue, some subsequent cryptocurrencies experimented with stepping away from the
proof-of-work system. To do this successfully, they needed
to come up with a setup that based on the information
from the previous transactions would automatically check
that proposed transactions are valid and add them to the

ledger. One innovation that was proposed to achieve this was *proof-of-stake* scheme, intended to complement, or even replace, the proof-of-work scheme. While proof-of-work awards the first party to come up with a solution to the hashing puzzle, proof-of-stake instead distributed the reward to all holders of a cryptocurrency, with people who hold more coins (i.e., those who have more stake in the system) receiving a larger "dividend." Similar to proof-of-work, proof-of-stake provides a measure of security for the system because it cannot be easily counterfeited. While the former requires substantial computations that would be difficult to reproduce for an attacker, the latter requires establishing large holdings of a cryptocurrency, which would not only be costly for an attacker to gather but also would align incentives with the rest of the system. Undermining currency is less attractive when one is holding a large stake in that currency.

The first cryptocurrency based on this idea was Peercoin, established in August 2012. Peercoin uses a mixture of proof-of-work, which allows it to mine coins much as Bitcoin does, and proof-of-stake, which would eventually replace proof-of-work when the cryptocurrency becomes more established. Peercoin's proof-of-stake is based on the concept of coin age, which accounts not only for how many coins network participants are holding but also for the time they have been holding these coins without earning the proof-of-stake dividend from their holdings. The Peercoin's proof-of-stake algorithm randomly selects the Peercoin holder who will mine the next block in the blockchain, with the probability of being chosen increasing in accord with the age of the coins that the person holds.[16] That person will then be able to create the next block in Peercoin's blockchain and get the reward for doing so. Importantly, the winner needs to be active on the network to do so—that is, Peercoin awards holders of its cryptocurrency, but only if such holders keep their computer online, ready to participate in the network and to help validate Peercoin transactions.

As Peercoin gains popularity, its creators plan to make it reliant exclusively on proof-of-stake, eliminating the need for proof-of-work and its potential negative effects. For the system to remain attractive, the total number of peercoins will be allowed to steadily increase (in contrast to the limited number of bitcoins), providing a continuing incentive for Peercoin users to participate in the network and earn their proof-of-stake rewards. Peercoin designers built in the steady 1 percent per year increase in the supply of peercoins into the cryptocurrency's algorithm.

Nxt

A more recent cryptocurrency that uses the proof-of-stake scheme is Nxt, established in November 2013. Its innovation is that the cryptocurrency is solely based on proof-of-stake and that it discards proof-of-work completely. Another interesting innovation in Nxt is that it keeps the money supply static, with all coins being premined and allocated across the initial users of the system. This means that all Nxt transactions must be accompanied by fees, which are then earned by the network nodes validating these transactions based on their proof-of-stake.

The proof-of-stake methods used in Peercoin and Nxt go a long way to solve the negative side effects of proof-of-work systems: excessive energy consumption and the mining arms race. The reason for that goes back to the economics of these systems and the incentives they create. As we saw earlier, the proof-of-work externalities have to do with the tournament structure of that system. In contrast, proof-of-stake does away with the tournament and simply selects the winner randomly based on the number of coins they hold. The winner will then need to engage in solving a cryptographic puzzle, but the puzzle is substantially easier than those currently being solved for Bitcoin and other cryptocurrencies based on proof-of-work. This means that the winner has little incentive to invest in state of the art computing systems. Moreover, there is no incentive for others to try to engage in any computation at all—the writer of the next block is assigned randomly, and you cannot improve your probability by investing in a newer mining rig or by proactively doing some calculations.

The probability of being chosen can be influenced by acquiring more coins. This illustrates a potential drawback of proof-of-stake systems: an entity that controls the majority of the currency will be selected more often than will anybody else, and thus the entity may acquire the power to take control of and potentially rewrite the blockchain. Some of these systems' proponents would argue that diffusing the currency across a large number of users would make these outcomes less likely, which is undoubtedly true. However, there are also additional security devices built into the algorithms. For example, Nxt uses "transparent forging," allowing network participants to monitor the randomly drawn nodes that are allowed to mine new blocks in the blockchain.

Novacoin
Overall, it seems that the proof-of-stake innovation is a clever and successful solution to the excessive energy consumption and mining arms race experienced by Bitcoin and similar cryptocurrencies. In the meantime, however, Peercoin at least remains largely reliant on proof-of-work (at the time of writing, 90 percent of the rewards are based

on proof-of-work rather than proof-of-stake) and suffers
from drawbacks similar to those of earlier cryptocurrencies.
For example, we see that ASIC machines that dominate
Bitcoin and Litecoin mining are increasingly used in Peercoin as well. The cryptocurrency community responded
similarly to this development as it did to Bitcoin: it created
a new altcoin. That new currency, Novacoin, was intro
duced in February 2013. It is closely related to Peercoin
in its design, but Novacoin uses scrypt, a hashing algorithm that at that time has not yet been dominated by
large-scale, ASIC-machine-based mining.

*   *   *

Our review of various altcoins has highlighted how their
designers addressed the flaws they saw in Bitcoin's design.
Litecoin and Feathercoin focused on changing the hashing
algorithm to improve energy consumption. Peercoin and
Novacoin took different approach to the energy issue by
adopting proof-of-stake. In addition to energy consumption, Peercoin and Novacoin tackled the limited supply
of currency. Overall, Litecoin, Feathercoin, Peercoin, and
Novacoin improve on Bitcoin and on each other by alleviating the problems of energy consumption, 51 percent attack,
and deflationary incentives. Out of this group, Novacoin
has arguably the most attractive attributes, and it may be
considered of highest promise from among considered
cryptocurrenices. Nonetheless, Bitcoin is the most popular. Litecoin is still quite active, but other cryptocurrencies,
especially Novacoin, are barely traded. The main reason
for this dynamic is likely network effects and the resulting
excess inertia. As we have seen in the history of currencies,
sometimes people are reluctant to adopt a new currency,
even one with more attractive attributes, if they worry that

other people may not adopt it as well. So, sometimes the expectations whether other people will use it may be more important than the currency's attributes. Indeed, among the considered group, the popularity and activity of a coin is more closely related to the age of the coin—that is, the date when it was started—than to the details of its design.

Anonymity Coins
Other altcoins attempted to improve on Bitcoin's design in a different dimension: anonymity. As we discussed above, Bitcoin is better characterized as a pseudonymous currency than as an anonymous currency. With enough resources, the real-life identity of Bitcoin's users can be unmasked, as in the Silk Road case. Consequently, a few altcoins tried to improve on protecting the users' privacy and increasing the anonymity of transactions. Of these, Dash and Cloakcoin are perhaps best known.

Dash was introduced as XCoin in January 2014. In February 2014, the name was changed to Darkcoin, and in March 2015, it was changed to Dash. It increases the anonymity by bundling transactions through a process called coin mixing. For example, instead of two separate transactions, from A to B and from X to Y, the ledger reflects only one transaction, from A and X to B and Y, obscuring the individual transaction links. The problem with straightforward coin mixing is that the transaction inputs and outputs can be matched by size. If A sends 2 Dash and X sends 5 Dash while B receives 2 Dash and Y receives 5 Dash, the transactions can be matched, even with coin mixing. Darkcoin countered it with premixing denominations already in the wallet and combining identical inputs, so that inputs cannot be matched to outputs. For example, A's wallet can send two independent transactions (and thus cannot be connected to the same sender), and X's wallet can send five independent transactions, 1 Dash each. With seven independent 1 Dash transactions, each received to a separate address, it cannot be seen directly that B received 2 Dash and X received 5 Dash.

Some people may worry though that coin mixing is not a sufficient guarantee of anonymity or that coin mixing still allows for tracing transactions. This may be because they do not believe that combining identical inputs is enough to prevent identifying by comparing inputs and outputs, or they worry that despite cost some entity— say, a government—could take control of a large number of masternodes and be able to trace the transactions. The anonymity attribute seems to be important enough for the community to continue new developments in this direction.

Cloakcoin, introduced in May 2014, further improves anonymity with a different system, a proof-of-stake anonymity, often referred to as PoSA. Instead of the more-common proof-of-work, it uses a modified proof-of-stake system, promising a 6 percent return for those who keep their digital wallets active online, ready to conduct verification of transactions. To ensure anonymity, each transaction uses a unique stealth address.

Cloakcoin's designers realize that to achieve anonymity in a transaction, it is not enough to assure the anonymity of the ledger, but anonymity is also needed for other elements of the ecosystem. Therefore, Cloakcoin's digital wallet is linked to a proprietary exchange that trades Cloakcoins, called CloakTrade. The exchange is decentralized and operates on a purely peer-to-peer basis.

Despite the improvements, however, none of these altcoins has become more popular than Bitcoin. It may again be due to excess inertia, or in this case, there may be also another reason: an insufficient number of people care about this particular attribute.

Tipping Coins

The cryptocurrencies we discussed above were based on earlier innovations and, directly or indirectly, on Bitcoin. But in each case, the currencies introduced a new element to the design. We discussed how these new elements influence the economics of these currencies.

At the same time, given that the basic cryptocurrency algorithm is in the public domain, it is easy to build a new altcoin with exactly the same design (and, hence, the same economics) but with a different branding. We discuss three examples of such cryptocurrencies: the Dogecoin, Karmacoin, and Reddcoin.

Dogecoin was created by Billy Markus and Jackson Palmer in December 2013. At the time, Bitcoin had gained substantial popularity and presence in the media. The interest was partly driven by the innovation of Bitcoin and the potential challenge to state-issued money, but some had more sensational origins, for example, the investigations of who Satoshi Nakamoto truly was or the Silk Road bust in the fall of 2013. This newly gained notoriety made Bitcoin an interesting concept to read or hear about but possibly not an innovation you would want to be a part of. Markus and Palmer wanted to change that, and they thought of a cryptocurrency design that would be more "fun to use." To make their altcoin more fun, they associated it with an image of a Shiba Inu dog. The name of the currency is also derived from a misspelled, or perhaps spelled in a cooler manner, word: "dog."

The cryptocurrency was proposed as a "tipping coin": available in large quantities, with a relatively low price per unit. The goal was to make it suitable for philanthropy, charity, and tipping—in essence, the equivalent of a "Like" or "+1" button that would convey a small monetary reward.

Of course, a similar tipping method could be designed using one of the earlier cryptocurrencies, say Bitcoin. However, the concern would have been that the negative aspects of Bitcoin's reputation would make people less likely to use the currency in this manner. To live up to its line "to do good and to feel good" Dogecoin needed to project a different image. It did so, literally. Moreover, the denomination matters psychologically: sending or receiving 100 dogecoins may well feel better than, say, sending or receiving 0.00006 bitcoins, even if the value of the gift is the same in the units of the state-issued currency, say, a dollar.

Dogecoin was designed with its intended use in mind. Its original algorithm was borrowed from the luckycoin, a "casino currency" that randomized the mining rewards, presumably to make using the currency more exciting for its users.[17] However, because this feature created uncertainty about the cost and benefits of mining, it did not catch on in the Dogecoin community. Consequently, in February 2014, the rewards for mining were set to the fixed amount of 250,000.

The total number of dogecoins to be created was initially thought to be fixed at a relatively large number (100 billion), promising enough units of the currency to support tipping. Due to a quirk (likely a mistake) in Dogecoin's programming, however, the algorithm was set to keep awarding a fixed number of dogecoins per block indefinitely, making the supply of the currency increasing over time and potentially unbounded. The Dogecoin community has decided not to remove this feature. One consequence of the higher total supply of the Dogecoin and of its higher award per block is that its value per coin is lower than is that of the Bitcoin. This fits well with the intended use of the cryptocurrency, for example tipping small monetary values in round units of the currency.

Dogecoin seems to have found a niche in the Internet economy. Much to the surprise of its early critics, it has won a sizeable following, and it has been incorporated into various websites. For example, in June 2014, Facebook approved Dogecoin tipping on its platform.[18]

Dogecoin is not the only coin that aims to promote philanthropy. Karmacoin (later renamed simply Karma) started in February 2014. Much like the Dogecoin, it is a "tipping coin" designed to allow its users to send small monetary values as a token of their appreciation and to "spread karma." Its design was initially very similar to Dogecoin, which by that time had already adopted deterministic rewards for mining. In June 2014, Karma underwent a substantial redesign, changing its hashing algorithm from scrypt (the same algorithm Litecoin adopted) to X11 and adding a proof-of-stake element to its reward system. These changes were likely economically motivated and served to differentiate Karma from its two direct competitors, Dogecoin and Reddcoin.

Reddcoin, the final "tipping coin" we describe here, has been branded as "social currency"—to be used with social networks to transfer money instantly and with zero transaction fees. Similar to Dogecoin and Karma, Reddcoin was intended to be used to express appreciation with money—in other words, to tip. Reddcoin also started with a design similar to that of Dogecoin, using the same proof-of-work system as Dogecoin and the same hashing algorithm. While the basic algorithm adopted in Reddcoin is relatively common, its design included some features that were oriented toward social interaction, for example, the Reddcoin digital wallet included the option of posting Twitter feeds.

In August 2014, Reddcoin went through an important change in its design, changing its proof-of-work approach to the newly developed proof-of-stake velocity (PoSV).[19] PoSV is based on the same idea as proof-of-stake, used in Peercoin. As an innovation, PoSV rewards participants in the Reddcoin ecosystem with newly issued coins. The original proof-of-stake system awards the new coins based on the holdings of the cryptocurrency—in essence, it pays a dividend—regardless of how actively one is using the currency. In contrast, PoSV rewards users not only for holding the coins but also for spending and receiving them. This ingenious innovation not only encourages ownership (stake) but also promotes activity (velocity). This helps align the incentives of the cryptocurrency's users with the usefulness and the potential of the overall scheme. PoSV makes it relatively more attractive to spend and earn reddcoins. This in turn makes it more likely that people will be active in the Reddcoin ecosystem, leading to greater network effects. For example, somebody who thinks about adopting a currency will evaluate how easy it will be to find others who are willing to use that currency while transacting with him. Everything else equal, it will be easier to find willing buyers and sellers in an ecosystem with PoSV.

Overall, even in the relatively narrow category of "tipping coins" we find a number of different currencies that have started with a very similar design and have aimed at a similar purpose. As with the other cryptocurrencies, here too we see rapid innovation and improvements to the initial algorithm, leading to increasing differences across the coins. Of these, PoSV, first adopted in Reddcoin, seems to be the most creative way of improving the economic prospects of the cryptocurrency.

The ongoing innovation notwithstanding, the first tipping coin, Dogecoin, remains the most significant, for example, in terms of its presence on cryptocurrency exchanges, the volume of trade, and so on. This is likely because Dogecoin is the oldest tipping coin, and perhaps it has had more traction early on and has had a chance to win a relatively larger following than the younger tipping coins. Again, the size of the network and the corresponding network effects and excess inertia determine the popularity of the cryptocurrency, even though some would argue that other, more recent innovations offer a relatively better design and functionality.

Copycat Cryptocurrencies

In our short review, we described a number of Bitcoin's cousins, focusing on those that introduced a particularly interesting innovation and those that may be the strongest competitors to Bitcoin and possibly to state-issued currencies.

This, however, merely scratches the surface. There are at present many hundreds of cryptocurrencies that are basically copies or clones of Bitcoin, Litecoin, or Peercoin. For example, Zetacoin and Monacoin are based on Bitcoin; Infinitecoin, Goldcoin, and Ekrona use Litecoin's design, and so on. These cryptocurrencies might differ from their predecessors in certain features of their technical design; for example, what hashing algorithm is used, how often new blocks are added to the blockchain, how many coins are rewarded per block, or whether they solely use proof-of-work or some combination of proof-of-work and proof-of-stake. As we discussed, these features have relatively little impact on the economics of these currencies, in terms of the incentives structure the features impose on the users and how they affect the system. From this point of view we might call these currencies, perhaps a bit harshly, copycat currencies.

The number of copycat currencies that have mushroomed over the last few years is surprising. These altcoins use the same technology and do not offer their users any meaningful improvement over the earlier ones. Moreover, the fact that the copycats are more recent means that they usually have a smaller network of users than the older cryptocurrencies do, and thus their usage is based on relatively weaker network effects. Overall, this means that copycat currencies are less likely than are their predecessors to become widely adopted. Why then are such copycat cryptocurrencies created, and what are the incentives of the people who mine them?

First, the costs of creating a new altcoin are very low. Since Bitcoin is open source, anyone can reuse the same algorithm and code to create a similar cryptocurrency. In fact, since changing the underlying code requires more expertise than simply copying it, it is easier and hence cheaper to produce a copycat currency than to create a cryptocurrency meaningfully different from its predecessors. A telling illustration of the ease of creating new altcoin is a now defunct website, Coingen.io, which allowed users to automatically generate an altcoin by choosing the desired settings for different attributes (e.g., how often a block is added to the blockchain, how many coins successful miners get, how quickly the reward for mining decreases).

If the costs are so low, what are the incentives and potential profits for people starting a new cryptocurrency or helping mine a copycat upstart? It has been suggested that some of these cryptocurrencies may actually be characterized as pump-and-dump schemes. Cryptocurrencies typically start with a number of coins that are already premined. That is, these coins are created before the first block on the blockchain and before the cryptocurrency is brought into the mining community. Later, as the miners mine new coins and sell them on the market, the owner of premined coins buys a lot of them, to increase the price. That's the "pump." With the increasing price, the altcoin attracts attention. As more people see it as a potential success, they might want to participate in it or even start viewing it as an investment. When they buy some units of the cryptocurrency, they typically buy them from the creators of the scheme, who choose this opportunity to cash out, by selling their stock of the altcoin. That's the "dump." Afterward, the price usually drops and never recovers.

Another and perhaps less controversial reason why copycat currencies are started is miners looking for alternatives. They may be discouraged from participating in the older schemes because they lack the specialized ASIC machines necessary to have a chance to be successful when mining bitcoins or litecoins. Instead, such miners may be looking for newer, less crowded altcoins to mine, because they stand a higher chance of successfully earning such currencies. They might then hope to sell such cryptocurrencies in digital exchanges.

Of course, the above argument only begs the question of why anybody would buy the copycat altcoins from such miners. It is possible that some people may trade them as an experiment, perhaps to get to know the industry, and they perceive such cryptocurrencies to be more accessible than, say, Bitcoin. Indeed, we often see such upstart currencies appear on cryptocurrency exchanges, and even though they typically fail to attract large volume of trade, they do occasionally transact.

Overall, while there has been a proliferation of crypto-currencies with a wide range of attributes, we generally see that older coins have an advantage over younger. Bitcoin, the oldest of them all, is still the most successful one among the cryptocurrencies. We can see this, for example, by comparing the market capitalization of the various currencies, that is, the number of coins outstanding multiplied by the price per coin. By that measure, Bitcoin's total market capitalization as of May 2015, about $3 billion US dollars, was many times larger than the market capitalization of Litecoin, the second most popular altcoin.

Bitcoin's success is likely linked to its first-mover advantage. As the first cryptocurrency, it has had the longest time to attract a larger following. It appears in the media the most. In terms of our earlier analyses, Bitcoin's dominance may well reflect excess inertia.

At the same time, a new cryptocurrency may overcome this initial disadvantage if it attracts a sufficiently large audience. It may be able to attract such audience either because it is overall technologically superior or because it is superior for a particular purpose. This means that the copycat currencies we discussed above seem to have little chance to become more widely accepted. Moreover, in line with these arguments, we do observe quality improvements, or at least attempts at such improvements, which may make a cryptocurrency more attractive to the general audience. We discussed such improvements in the context of Litecoin, Feathercoin, Peercoin, and Novacoin—although so far none of these currencies managed to challenge Bitcoin significantly.

In parallel, we see the development of altcoins optimized for a particular purpose. For example, we saw currencies such as Dash or Cloakcoin, designed to improve the protection of their users' privacy, or coins designed for tipping and low-value charitable transfers, for example, Dogecoin, Karma, or Reddcoin. These cryptocurrency systems may attract their following by focusing on such a narrow niche and servicing it well.

4.6. MORE THAN JUST A CURRENCY

So far, we have focused on cryptocurrencies that are designed to serve as an equivalent of cash in the digital universe. These cryptocurrencies are ultimately based on Bitcoin and its ingenious way of solving the double-spending problem. However, it turns out that the solution proposed by Satoshi Nakamoto is not limited to digital currencies. The concept of blockchain can be generalized to a wide range of other applications.

Namecoin was introduced in 2010 with the goal of improving anonymity of Internet activity, for example, to protect voices of dissidents. The Namecoin system is a decentralized hosting of the web domain ".bit," so that no entity can take control and shut down a website, in contrast to regular domains, facilitated by ICANN—Internet Corporation for Assigned Names and Numbers. The Namecoin system uses native currency, denominated in namecoins, for payments to obtain or renew a website in the .bit domain through the Namecoin blockchain. In terms of currency design, however, namecoins do not differ from bitcoins. In fact, they can be mined concurrently in the same process.

Another blockchain innovation is Ethereum, a system that was designed in 2011 and released in 2015. Ethereum is described by its developers as "a platform for decentralized applications." It uses a similar technology to other cryptocurrencies, but instead of creating a decentralized network to send transactions, it aims to build a network that would support Ethereum contracts. These contracts would provide services such as content publication, dynamic messaging, and transactions, but in a fully decentralized and pseudonymous way.

Ethereum can be thought of as a framework or a language in which smart contracts can be written. These contracts are applications that have their own rules for ownership, transactions, and so on. These smart contracts may find application in a number of settings, ranging from voting systems to intellectual property to financial exchanges.

The concepts of blockchain and decentralized ledger can also be used with protocols other than Bitcoin's. The best known such alternative system is Ripple. Ripple is a payment network developed by Ripple Labs, a Vancouver company formerly known as OpenCoin, now relocated to San Francisco. The company developed the Ripple to facilitate trade in various currencies (crypto- and state-issued ones); for example, to allow cross-border remittances that would be cheaper than are those available from traditional providers such as banks or Western Union. The Ripple payment system was launched in 2011.

The Ripple network introduces a decentralized, open ledger that records participants' offers to trade various currencies. To execute trade, the system uses intermediate cryptocurrency, XRP, also called "ripples." Unlike most other cryptocurrencies, the pool of ripples is already premined: the currency is available for sale from Ripple Labs itself or from private parties, but new ripples cannot be generated by the equivalent of Bitcoin mining. The way that this intermediate currency works harks back to the medieval system of transferring money through IOUs issued by financial intermediaries. In those days, you would deposit your cash with an intermediary and collect their IOU. You could then hand the IOU to another intermediary, perhaps in a different geographic region, and collect your cash back. Traveler's checks are a more modern invention that works in a very similar manner.

When you want to use Ripple to transfer currency, you approach a node in the Ripple network with your request. That node finds a node at your desired destination. In practice, there may be a chain of intermediate nodes between the two. Instead of sending them your cash, which would be time consuming and would need to use the infrastructure of traditional financial institutions, the origin node sends XRP equivalent of your cash to the destination node. The destination node then can exchange the ripples into the currency desired at that end of the transaction. By bypassing much of the traditional financial infrastructure, Ripple promises that such transfers or exchanges would be low cost relative to traditional services.

By its design, the Ripple network may be more attractive for financial institutions than for individual consumers. Since a consumer would need to find a Ripple node to be able to use the system, it may be easier if such nodes were located at the bank of the consumer's choice. The benefit for the bank is that the Ripple network would give it a global coverage and the ability to send real-time payments. Thus, Ripple does not position itself as a competitor to Bitcoin or other cryptocurrencies, or to state-issued currencies.[20]

Ripple has gained substantial popularity over the last few years. Its currency, XRP, has gained a substantial market capitalization. As of May 2015, it was around $200 million US dollars, about three times as much as Litecoin, but still substantially less than Bitcoin's $3 billion.

Perhaps a more persuasive testimony of Ripple's popularity is that it is being adopted by institutions in the traditional financial system interested in modernizing their payment networks. The first institution to integrate the Ripple protocol was Fidor, a German bank, which did so in 2011. A few months later, two US banks, CBW Bank and Cross River Bank, followed suit.

4.7. Trading Cryptocurrencies

So far, we discussed how money facilitates exchange, implicitly assuming that people who want to use it already have the currency from some source. We also covered one such source of cryptocurrencies: mining. However, few potential users of, say, Bitcoin, can reliably get that currency from mining. As we explained, mining has become ultracompetitive, and it requires substantial resources and expertise from anybody who wants to do it successfully. Similarly, you may earn bitcoins if you are a merchant and accept payment for your product in that currency. However, few people would want to start a business solely to acquire bitcoins to then spend them on a different good.

Fortunately, there are easier ways to acquire cryptocurrencies such as Bitcoin: you can buy them from other people. "Buying" cryptocurrencies is conceptually similar to exchanging units of one state-issued currency (say, the dollar) for another (say, the pound). In this chapter, we overview various ways of performing such transactions, with the focus on online exchanges that allow such trades. If cryptocurrencies were to be widely adopted, exchanges like these would become important features of the financial system. Without them, large-scale flows between cryptocurrencies such as Bitcoin and other currencies (both crypto- and state-issued ones) would be difficult, which would be a major impediment for cryptocurrencies to play a role in the economy.

Before we move on to exchanges, a simple way for an average person to acquire a cryptocurrency is to find a seller directly. Such meet-ups were the oldest way for people to acquire bitcoins without having to become miners themselves. Usually, people interested in trading would coordinate over the Internet, using message boards and email. They would then meet "in the real world" and transact. The buyer would provide the state-issued currency, and the seller would initiate the Bitcoin transfer.

The above description likely reminds you of an early form of exchange: barter. The problem associated with barter, coincidence of wants, arises here as well. If you'd like to buy bitcoins, you first need to find someone willing to part with them for the amount of state-issued currency that both of you find acceptable. Of course, modern technology makes this problem much easier to solve than it has been historically, but it is a friction nonetheless. One of the themes in our book is that such frictions spur innovation and catalyze new, improved designs. This time is no different: Bitcoin ATMs have appeared in a few countries, allowing for an easy exchange of the state-issued currency for bitcoins.

Bitcoin Automatic Teller Machines (often referred to as BTMs) allow users to exchange state-issued cash for bitcoins without having to find a willing seller and arrange a meeting with him or her. The first such machine was introduced in October 2013 in Vancouver, Canada. Over the past few years, BTMs have been introduced in countries ranging from Argentina to the United States, making them an increasingly popular, but perhaps still a somewhat exotic, sight. Initially, these BTMs allowed users to purchase bitcoins only, and BTMs were not designed to allow users to sell their bitcoins for state-issued currencies. Most BTM still have this limitation. Recently, however, some two-way BTMs appeared as well, where one can both buy and sell bitcoins.[21]

Both personal meet-ups and BTMs may satisfy the average person's demand for a cryptocurrency, but they could hardly serve the wider economy. For example, it would be uneconomical for larger merchants to try to identify private parties ready to exchange their revenues from and into bitcoins or for such merchants to make frequent trips to a BTM. For the economy to run smoothly, we need a way to conduct more wholesale transactions. Online cryptocurrency exchanges provide one such way.

An online cryptocurrency exchange is a two-sided platform that connects buyers and sellers and allows them to trade their cryptocurrency holdings. Conceptually, it is similar to a traditional financial exchange, and it gives users an opportunity to deploy strategies similar to those that one would deploy in, say, a stock market. For example, you could transact your cryptocurrency at the price prevailing at a given moment but also post limit orders—that is, instruct the exchange to buy or sell on your behalf in the future, as long as the price becomes cheap enough or expensive enough. Exchanges are also commonly linked to the traditional financial system, allowing users to fund their accounts with state-issued currencies to then acquire cryptocurrencies, or conversely, to sell their cryptocurrencies and then withdraw the state-issued currency from the exchange. Importantly, exchanges usually do not buy or sell cryptocurrencies on their own account; they just match buyers and sellers. Exchanges are simply intermediaries that provide the service of matching buyers and sellers willing to transact at a given price.

The landscape of cryptocurrency exchanges is still young and very dynamic. We see new entrants competing with longer established exchanges, often successfully, leading to frequent changes in the ranking of the most active exchanges. Below we give a quick historical background on Mt. Gox—probably the exchange best known to the public and also one of the most important for development of Bitcoin trading.

Mt. Gox was a Tokyo-based exchange that had been the most important Bitcoin exchange in the first years of Bitcoin's existence. By some estimates, Mt. Gox was responsible for handling 90 percent of Bitcoin trades, clearly dominating this market. Its size and importance attracted not only users willing to trade bitcoins but also attackers. In 2011, the exchange had been compromised by a hacker who managed to manipulate the site and the bitcoin price it listed and who succeeded in sending him- or herself a large number of bitcoins obtained at the artificially depressed price. Mt. Gox recovered from the attack, but its temporary weakness caused it to lose market share to competitors.

In spite of its problems, Mt. Gox remained the dominant Bitcoin exchange until mid-2013. In early 2013, it became difficult for US customers to access Mt. Gox. Historically, US customers were served using a bank account that belonged to a Mt. Gox subsidiary, but in May 2013, that account was frozen by the FBI. Over the next few months, the balance tipped, and while Mt. Gox remained an important exchange, it lost its dominant position and only controlled about 27 percent of the market. Its remaining market share was divided between the Chinese exchange BTC China (35 percent of Bitcoin trades), Bitstamp (24 percent), and BTC-e (14 percent). Each of these exchanges had its own specific rules, for example,

BTC China only allowed trades of Bitcoin against the Chinese yuan, whereas the remaining exchanges allowed trading Bitcoin versus the US dollar.

Over the subsequent few months, new exchanges appeared (e.g., China's OKCoin, which grew to be one of the largest exchanges as of the time of writing); others disappeared from the market, most notably, Mt. Gox itself. In February 2014, the exchange was again attacked by hackers, and this time the attack has proven to be crippling. According to estimates, $350 million worth of bitcoins were lost (possibly stolen), leading to the shutdown of the exchange.

After the Mt. Gox shutdown, the Bitcoin market was in turmoil; predictably, the exchange rate of the cryptocurrency versus state-issued currencies fell. Nonetheless, the market proved to be remarkably resilient, and new exchanges appeared to fill the vacuum left by the disappearance of Mt. Gox. As of the writing of this book, Bitcoin can be traded on about 100 different online exchanges, many of which also allow trading a number of other cryptocurrencies.

Gandal and Halaburda (2014) provide a glimpse at the economics of the online cryptocurrency exchanges. The paper focuses on BTC-e, one of the largest exchanges at the time that allowed trades in a number of cryptocurrencies, including seven particularly popular ones that we know from the earlier chapters: Bitcoin, Litecoin, Peercoin, Namecoin, Feathercoin, Novacoin, and Terracoin. To check the robustness of their findings, the researchers also analyzed Cryptsy, another popular exchange.

An economic analysis of exchanges not only helps us understand how well cryptocurrencies work as part of the overall economy in terms of the quality of the financial infrastructure—for example the exchanges themselves—but also helps us gauge how much attention people pay to the various cryptocurrencies. For example, in a well-functioning market, prices on the exchange should reflect all information available about each cryptocurrency. It is actually fairly difficult to test how efficient markets are from that perspective. In fact, people still argue about the efficiency of markets in the traditional financial system. However, whether the market is more or less efficient, it is generally agreed that a market should not allow what economists call "arbitrage opportunities." Arbitrage is a type of trade that guarantees an investor instantaneous profit for sure, without the investor taking on any risk. In well-functioning markets, arbitrage opportunities should arise only accidentally. To the extent they do arise in practice, they are usually caused by market fragmentation, a particular friction in the way people trade, or perhaps are just a testimony that the market is relatively small and that its participants do not pay enough attention to what is happening in it.

We can illustrate an arbitrage opportunity with a simple example. Suppose that you log into an online cryptocurrency exchange that allows you to buy or sell one bitcoin for $250. If you wanted to trade litecoins instead, you could buy or sell a litecoin for $2 each. Last, you may decide to trade the two cryptocurrencies directly against each other, without resorting to the US dollars. For such a trade, suppose that the quoted exchange rate is 100 litecoins per bitcoin.

It turns out that the prices in our example are not internally consistent, and this presents an arbitrage opportunity to a smart trader. Here's how you can take advantage of this opportunity. Suppose you buy 100 litecoins for $200, using the second exchange rate in the above paragraph. As soon as that transaction is done, you can buy one bitcoin for your newly gained 100 litecoins, as per the third exchange rate above. Finally, you can sell your bitcoin for $250 using the first exchange rate. Your total profit from the transaction is then $50—the difference between your initial investment of $200 and the total payoff from selling bitcoin at $250. This type of arbitrage, popular in foreign exchange investments, is often called "triangular arbitrage," because it takes three exchange rates to execute it.

You might consider $50 a decent payment for a moment's work. (Remember, you are trying to execute these trades as quickly as you can—if you wait for too long, you risk that the prices change and the opportunity disappears.) It principle, however, the arbitrage opportunity may lead to substantially higher profits. To maximize your profits, a trader would try to buy as many litecoins as possible, exchange them into bitcoins, and finally exchange all the bitcoins into dollars. As market participants catch on to the opportunity, they start trading in this manner, pushing prices until they adjust to the levels that will eliminate the arbitrage opportunity (e.g., until litecoin will become more expensive or bitcoin will become cheaper).

The strategy we described above is relatively simple, so should we expect to see this in reality? Such triangular arbitrage is extremely rare in traditional foreign exchange markets, where a crowd of traders, both human and computer, pays close attention to the prices and acts as soon as the prices deviate from no-arbitrage levels. However, Gandal and Halaburda (2014) showed that we do see such arbitrage opportunities in the cryptocurrency markets, suggesting they are not nearly as well developed as we could hope.

Gandal and Halaburda analyzed a few different currency triples. Their first test dealt with exchange rates that linked the most popular currencies: the US dollar, Bitcoin, and Litecoin. They find no evidence of arbitrage on average, suggesting that the exchange works well most of the time. However, it still sometimes fails to operate efficiently. It turns out that about 2 percent of the time these exchange rates allowed for a triangular arbitrage opportunity, yielding returns greater than 1.4 percent. While the magnitude of the returns may seem low, note that this is a potentially riskless return that a trader may earn over a very short period of time. Even if the arbitrage opportunity is eliminated relatively quickly, the rate of return is much more attractive compared with most other investments.

The evidence of profitable arbitrage opportunities turned out to be stronger for cryptocurrencies that are less popular than Bitcoin is—Peercoin and Namecoin. For these currencies, about 2 percent of the time the potential profits exceeded 2 percent of capital invested, indicating that the trading opportunities between Peercoin and Namecoin were more attractive than those between Bitcoin and Litecoin. This likely reflects the differences in the interest these cryptocurrencies generate and the relative liquidity of their market that is the consequence of this interest: In general, we expect more liquid markets to provide fewer triangular trading opportunities.

Another type of arbitrage that is possible with multiple exchanges is cross-exchange arbitrage. That is, suppose that bitcoins are available at the exchange rate of $240 per bitcoin at one exchange but at $250 per bitcoin at another one. This again provides opportunities for riskless profit: a trader could buy bitcoins at the lower price on the first exchange, then sell them at the higher price on the second, pocketing the difference. Again, traders would have incentive to keep on doing that until their buying and selling pressure equalizes the prices on the two exchanges.

Gandal and Halaburda (2014) investigate the occurrence of such an arbitrage between the BTC-e and Bitstamp exchanges. As before, there is little evidence of systematic arbitrage opportunities—in other words, if there are differences in rates quoted at the various exchanges, these differences do not arise all the time. Again, however, the researchers found evidence of meaningful deviations some of the time. For example, they found that on half of the trading days that they analyzed, the difference in Bitcoin–US dollar exchange rates differed by more than 2 percent across the two exchanges. The potential for opportunistic trading was even higher when the researchers analyzed Litecoin, a widely traded but less well-known cryptocurrency than Bitcoin.

Gandal and Halaburda used data on cryptocurrency prices recorded at midnight Greenwich Mean Time, effectively working only with one snapshot of data per day. Their data also covered only two large exchanges. This means that their analysis likely understates the possibility of arbitrage—there may have been more attractive opportunities at different times of the day or between other exchanges than those that they have analyzed.

The existence of cryptocurrency exchanges is also important for the competition across the various cryptocurrencies. The prices at which they trade on the exchanges can be interpreted as the market's assessment of the relative importance and value of each cryptocurrency. Given the importance of the network effects, this value depends on the assessment of which currency is more likely to win widespread adoption not only in the cryptocurrency market but perhaps also in the traditional segment of the economy.

In the aforementioned paper, Gandal and Halaburda investigate this question using price data from the exchanges. Their results illustrate interesting dynamics in the market's view of the various cryptocurrencies. In the earlier part of their sample, the researchers found evidence of the winner-take-all effects that we discussed earlier in the book. During that period, as Bitcoin became more valuable against the US dollar, it at the same time became more valuable against other cryptocurrencies. One interpretation of this pattern is that it reflects market participants' assessment of whether the market might eventually tip in Bitcoin's favor. As the probability of that event increases, Bitcoin becomes more valuable versus the state-issued currency (i.e., its price increases) but also versus the other cryptocurrencies that it might replace in the future.

Interestingly, in the more recent part of the sample in Gandal and Halaburda (2014), this pattern reverses. As Bitcoin becomes more expensive in terms of US dollars, it actually becomes cheaper when measured in units of other cryptocurrencies. At the end of the sample period (February 2014), Bitcoin is stronger against the US dollar and weaker against other top cryptocurrencies than it was at the beginning of the period. Thus, we no longer see winner-take-all dynamics. It might be that at that time the interest in cryptocurrencies overall grew so strongly that the increased demand pushed up all their prices, and the price of Bitcoin, the best known cryptocurrency, went up the least. The drivers of this increased demand are probably varied. They may include both the growing acceptance of cryptocurrencies and the increased confidence that one of them will be more widely adopted in the economy. Another driver of demand may be speculation: the hope of discovering "the next Bitcoin" may have

spurred people to invest more in alternative cryptocurrencies, pushing their prices higher than the Bitcoin's. We do
not have additional evidence corroborating either of these
channels, but the tone of the media articles from that
time suggests that both may have been operating at the
same time.

4.8. HOW DO CRYPTOCURRENCIES'
ATTRIBUTES COMPARE WITH
EARLIER MONEY?

Since Bitcoin's design aims to create a digital version of
cash, it is natural to ask how it compares with traditional
currencies on their most important characteristics, which
we reviewed in Chapter 2. This is particularly relevant
for any discussion of the competition between Bitcoin
and such currencies, not just to answer the question of
whether it is "better" but also to debate whether it is
"good enough" to fulfill some or all of the functions
traditional money serves today. While we consider these
questions from the point of view of Bitcoin, the discussion in this chapter also applies to other cryptocurrencies,
including those that attempted to fix some of Bitcoin's
shortcomings.

We saw that one of the relevant characteristics of money
is divisibility. Here, Bitcoin compares very favorably with
state-issued currencies, which typically operate using the
metric system and are divisible up to a hundredth of a
unit.[22] In contrast, Bitcoin allows precision to the eighth
decimal place, with its smallest unit named "satoshi" after
the inventor of the system. This provides for more divisibility and a higher precision not only than state-issued
currencies but also than measuring barley or metal by

weight. This enhanced divisibility may be particularly useful for micropayments.

Another characteristic is durability, that is, how long a currency can last. Again, the advantage here goes to Bitcoin. Bitcoins do not wear out or deteriorate. Of course, one can lose bitcoins. The media has reported a number of stories of people throwing away hard drives, or deleting wallets, and thus losing private keys that give them access to their bitcoins. The bitcoins, however, are still on the blockchain, and they will be there for as long as the Bitcoin network operates. From the point of view of the network, it is impossible to distinguish between a bitcoin that has been lost and a bitcoin the owner of which has not yet decided to spend it. In contrast, you can lose a bill (or even a coin) permanently by destroying them or damaging them to the point that they are no longer recognizable.

The bitcoins, being digital, are also easy to carry. There is of course the need for the software and hardware that manages them, for example, a digital wallet on your smartphone. Is this easier or more difficult than carrying cash or a credit card? That may depend on the person.

Storing bitcoins does not need to involve physical safes and security, but one needs encrypted digital storage to keep bitcoins safe. This is illustrated by implosions of a number of services offering storage of bitcoins. The most spectacular of those was likely Mt. Gox, mentioned earlier. Storing bitcoins safely may be easier or cheaper than keeping cash safe at home, but it is likely more complex than using credit cards and bank deposits. Banks or payment services providers tend to be more reliable than storing bitcoins, due to their experience, well-developed systems, and the insurance they offer directly or indirectly.

Of course, as the Bitcoin system matures one may imagine development of more secure storage options and services. Bitcoin is still a young currency, and one could argue that banks were not particularly safe early in their history due to theft from the outside and fraud from the inside.

As for the ease of transfer, it depends both on the available technology (e.g., access to computers or smart-phones) and on the ecosystem (e.g., interface). When relying directly on the basic Bitcoin system, transfers are cumbersome. They are more difficult than handling cash for person-to-person transactions, or using credit cards for long-distance transactions. You might compare using Bitcoin network directly with weighing metal to settle transactions. This historical system of unminted metal was cumbersome and required additional sophistication, which created additional transaction costs and was eventually eliminated by the introduction of coins. Similarly, the Bitcoin ecosystem is being developed, and a range of digital wallets has appeared, making it easier for Bitcoin users to transact.

Finally, unlike cash, bitcoin cannot be counterfeited, so if you get it in a transaction, you can rest easy that it is genuine.[23] Bitcoins may be stolen, but the transactions are not reversible (unlike credit cards), so this is not a concern for the seller.[24] Moreover, no person or institution can manipulate the supply of bitcoins, as it is managed by an algorithm.

Thus, on some dimensions it is not clear whether cryptocurrencies have more convenient attributes than the traditional currencies do. Whether it is easier to carry and transfer or safer to store may depend on the preferences of the users. But on other dimensions, they provide a clear improvement, like divisibility, durability, or risk or fraud and counterfeiting. Those attributes could make cryptocurrencies more useful for some uses, like micropayments or remote international payments, than older alternatives are. But the benefit needs to be large enough for people to adopt it and use it alongside (or instead of) the traditional banking system and credit card system.

4.9. COMPETITION AGAINST STATE-ISSUED CURRENCIES

The flurry of new cryptocurrencies we described above illustrates how intense the competition among these new currencies is. At the same time, an equally interesting and perhaps a more important question is the competition between cryptocurrencies (or a single cryptocurrency that might win the fight discussed above) and state-issued fiat currencies. The tools we developed so far in this book will allow us to analyze this question.

The key issues related to the potential widespread adoption of cryptocurrencies (or one particular cryptocurrency) are network effects and overcoming excess inertia that currently benefits state-issued currencies. We discussed both these concepts in the previous chapters. From this point of view, the plethora of cryptocurrencies may well be a problem. As we saw, individual cryptocurrencies have their advantages and likely proponents who would prefer those currencies over other cryptocurrencies. While this may well improve the quality of the whole category and lead to further innovations, such splintering of the market limits the network effects that any one cryptocurrency enjoys.

There are two broad reasons why this is detrimental to cryptocurrencies competing with state-issued currencies. First, and most directly, the more different cryptocurrencies

there are, and the more diverse the preferences of their
proponents, the more difficult it is for any one of them to
accrue the critical mass of users to position the currency
well against state-issued currencies. With fewer potential
buyers and sellers, there are lower incentives for everybody
else to start using the cryptocurrency. The fixed costs of
embracing a new currency can be substantial. The biggest
cost may involve adopting the technical infrastructure necessary for using the cryptocurrency. For buyers, this may
require obtaining a digital wallet for the currency, finding a
way to exchange state-issued currencies for the cryptocurrency, and so on. Sellers would additionally need to find a
way to incorporate the cryptocurrency in their accounting
systems, price their goods in the units of the cryptocurrency, possibly allow for the seamless transmission of both
crypto- and state-issued currencies between suppliers and
other business partners, and so on. Moreover, new users
need to learn to use the new cryptocurrency. They may
not be interested in the details of how it works, but they
need to understand how to use the software that allows
them to spend it, how to think about their wallet that now
combines various types of currencies, and so on.

These costs increase when there are multiple cryptocurrencies that may be used in the marketplace. While the
cost of acquiring a second or third cryptocurrency, or link-
ing them to your digital wallet, are relatively lower than
are the costs of the very first one, such costs exists nonetheless and make it more difficult to persuade people to
use the currency. Users that only opt for one currency are
not able to transact with merchants that may not allow
this particular one. While there may be intermediaries who
will seamlessly translate one cryptocurrency to another for
the purposes of a transaction, such a service would require

effort or maybe a fee from the user, which will further increase the costs of using the cryptocurrency.

The second broad issue is that the multiplicity of cryptocurrencies creates uncertainty that may delay the development of that market or stop people from joining it. For example, users who may potentially be interested in using cryptocurrencies may prefer to wait for the market to tip to one of them before adopting a cryptocurrency and risking that it will fail. An analogy that is useful here is the battle between the two high definition DVD formats, HD DVD and Blu-ray, which arguably held up the whole category.[25]

Of course, the competition between a cryptocurrency and the state-issued currency also depends on the relative attractiveness of the two—that is, on their efficiency in facilitating transactions and acting as money. We have already discussed how cryptocurrencies' basic attributes compare with traditional money attributes, along the dimensions considered in Chapter 2. But what matters in the end is whether these attributes make the currency sufficiently desirable for a sufficiently large group of people. That means that the new currency must be significantly better than the existing alternatives for some particular purpose.

Cryptocurrencies have some advantages over state-issued money. The most obvious are the ones exposed in Satoshi Nakamoto's paper that gave rise to Bitcoin: the ability to make online payments in a cheap way, allowing for micropayments because of its divisibility, and giving users a measure of anonymity. Some of these attributes can have both positive and negative impact. For example, anonymity may be viewed as a benefit over credit and ATM cards. It protects your privacy and may help you avoid fraud: you're not sending your card number, your address, or even your name to a merchant who might turn out to be dishonest. This may be particularly relevant when you transact with sellers in other countries, perhaps ones that do not provide you with the same protection as your home country. In those cases, you might decide not to transact if you had only a credit card at your disposal, but you may be more inclined to use cryptocurrencies to trade. Anonymity may also be important for dissidents in authoritarian regimes or, for example, for women in countries like Afghanistan, where they are legally not allowed to have a separate bank account. On the other hand, anonymity may also stimulate nefarious uses, as in the example of Silk Road discussed earlier.

There are other attributes of cryptocurrencies that are sometimes mentioned as advantages over cash but that are not as clear as the ones above. For example, it has been often pointed out that Bitcoin transactions are quicker and cheaper. But this description may be misleading. Bitcoin transactions typically take about 10 minutes to an hour to verify and settle, as a block is added every 10 minutes. Moreover, the transactions may require a fee of a small fraction of a bitcoin; otherwise, the verification of transaction may take longer. So whether it is quicker and cheaper depends on what do we compare it with. Its attributes make Bitcoin quicker and cheaper for merchants than credit cards are,[26] but this is not necessarily so for the customers.[27] And it is difficult to argue to what extent Bitcoin transactions are quicker than are cash transactions. Cash transactions are settled the moment the cash is handed over. It is hard to imagine someone rummaging through his or her wallet for longer than 10 minutes. It is possible, though, that Bitcoin transactions are cheaper than cash transactions are if one accounts the cost of going to the bank with cash to deposit it and the risk that it may be stolen on the way.

Overall, Bitcoin and other cryptocurrencies offer a number of novel and attractive attributes. The big question, however, is whether people would care enough to switch. Even if they do, the question then is whether enough people would care to create a critical mass of adopters to make it a viable currency.

CHAPTER 5

THE ROAD AHEAD

The twenty-first century's information technology has created a new context for the creation of (digital) money. This new environment provides never before seen flexibility for the design of currencies as well as unparalleled scale for their introduction. It is not surprising therefore that the beginning of the century has been marked by unprecedented experimentation with digital currencies, whether carried out by individuals, small startups, or large Internet businesses. The goals of these experiments have been as diverse as their approaches to solving the multitude of challenges that any large-scale payment system presents. Indeed, one of our objectives was to review these various motivations and the multitude of solutions proposed to address them. What patterns emerge from this dynamic picture?

First, experimentation is far from over for a variety of reasons, ranging from purely technological challenges (e.g., how to make "mining" efficient and cost effective for decentralized cryptocurrencies?) to regulatory ones (e.g., will governments restrict the use of digital currencies?), with many additional challenges in between. Second, and more important, consumers will continue to get accustomed to these innovations and may eventually start treating them as viable payment tools rather than something you just read about in the media. As hundreds of years of monetary history have taught us, the use of any currency is built on trust and, as of today, there is simply too little experience with any of the digital currencies for them to build universal trust. This is not to say that some of these currencies are not trusted by small communities (e.g., Bitcoin users on the Darknet) or by very large groups of people in restricted domains (e.g., potential millions of people using Amazon Coins). But none of these digital currencies rivals the trust in mainstream state-issued currencies. In this respect, a key issue is that the very flexibility and scale that digital currencies promise also bring increased risk for users, especially if they are used broadly.

Yet, taking a step back, it might be unreasonable to put digital currencies up to such a high standard. Another lesson history teaches us is that currencies have always coexisted—and usually, not just a few ones. In most developed economies, there are multitudes of restricted payment systems, all linked together in a complex web, for example, food stamps or BerkShares in the United States. This is also true if one takes a global perspective. Internationally, the multitude of state-issued currencies are overshadowed by a few particularly strong currencies—usually called reserve currencies because central banks may hold their exchange reserves in them. In a similar vein, why not expect digital currencies to proliferate and coexist in multiple forms alongside the state-issued currencies that we will continue to use?

Taking this perspective, we will likely see many forms of centralized currencies in use. As digital platforms develop, they will continue to experiment with digital currencies to better serve their business models. These experiments may be limited in time, only serving a temporary objective, as is the case of Amazon Coin, which can be thought of as a promotional tool to build the company's e-reader ecosystem in the face of aggressive competition. Some such currencies may be discontinued because the platform has grown in its activities, covering the trade of a much larger spectrum of products and services, which in turn justifies the use of the state-issued currency. This seems to be the case of China's Tencent, whose business has evolved from being a PC-based social network into becoming a general-purpose social e-commerce platform on mobile technology, called WeChat. A similar evolution seems to be under way at Facebook, the world's largest social network today. In sum, we do not expect much slowdown in the introduction of various centralized platform-based currencies.

More convergence is likely to happen in the world of cryptocurrencies. As these strive to be general-purpose global currencies, they may have a harder time to find a niche where they would have a clear advantage over existing alternatives for a sufficient number of people. However, it may be possible to have a handful of successful currencies coexisting, each with a critical mass of users. For these decentralized currencies, the network effects discussed earlier are of much more importance.

An important question is whether cryptocurrencies will drive state-issued currencies out of business. They may have the potential to do so, especially for state-issued currencies that have lost credibility with their citizens. Yet again, for most state-issued currencies, this is unlikely to happen. Put simply, governments have a lot of power to make the state-issued currency attractive to their citizens as long as it is backed with a sound monetary policy.

Finally, will governments outlaw digital currencies? They certainly are able do so in the case of platform-based currencies. In fact, they can ban the entire platform, as China did with Facebook, for example. Yet, it is not clear what purpose this might serve, given the fact that platform-based currencies are typically limited in some of their functionalities, therefore representing limited threat to the fully equipped state-issued currency. How about cryptocurrencies? Again, theoretically, governments can ban them, but the decentralized nature of cryptocurrencies makes this practically difficult or even impossible to enforce. Therefore, the relevant question is whether people will see utility in using a cryptocurrency in parallel with the state-issued currency.

Where does this all bring us? We went on a whirlwind tour of the exciting and dynamically evolving digital currency landscape. We approached these innovations as an economist would: by studying the roles they play in the marketplace, the incentives they present to their users, and the competition between various digital and state-issued currencies. This framework helps us to analyze what has happened in this space so far and gives us insight into what is yet to come. The biggest question of all, of course, is whether the world will tilt towards a purely digital currency in the future. This has not happened yet, and our analysis suggests why. Strong network effects and excess inertia strongly favor traditional instruments, which also satisfy most economic needs fairly well. Most, but not all economic needs: we highlighted some uses where digital currencies may well find a niche; for example, micropayments or cross-border remittances. There is ongoing competition for these segments of the marketplace, and it promises to be a fascinating spectacle.

Notes

Chapter 1

1. Independent of finance, the rise of the Internet has generally allowed people to more effectively question the authority of governments in many other respects. This phenomenon is not that different from earlier instances in history marked by the rise of major media technologies, for example, printing or radio.
2. See MarketWatch, "With Amazon minting currency, Fed at risk," www.marketwatch.com/story/could-amazon-run -central-banks-out-of-business-2013-02-13.

Chapter 2

1. For a comprehensive history, see e.g., Martin (2014), Ferguson (2008), Weatherford (1997).
2. See Harari (2015).
3. See Jevons (1875), Kiyotaki and Wright (1989).
4. See Paul Einzig (1966).
5. See e.g., Weatherford (1997).
6. That did not stop people from trying to get an unfair edge in a transaction. The most obvious example of dishonestly manipulating coins is debasement. It is not certain when this procedure started, although some sources point to the reign of the Roman emperor Nero (see Comparette, 1914). In the face of such manipulation, people weighted the coins again. It was only king's illusion that this would solve anything, because people used the underlying value of the metal to assess the value of the coin. But even then, at a given time, the value of a particular coin was well known, and trade was easier than with random pieces of metal.

7. In practice, however, it was not exercised in the United States after 1933, as owning gold was illegal for Americans between 1933 and 1974.
8. See Weatherford (1997).
9. For example, French Banque Royale in 1716–1720, issuance of Continentals during American Revolution, or Confederate dollars during the Civil War in US.
10. In our brief historical overview, we ignore a number of novel institutions, most importantly banks. For an overview of the evolution and the role of the banking system, see e.g., Ferguson (2008).
11. See Sheck (2008).
12. Notice that "store of value" in the definition does not mean we need money for saving. For saving, we can "invest in something" instead. In fact, money can be inconvenient to keep as savings exactly for the same reason it is money. If it is handy, easy to carry and exchange, then it is also easy to steal. This is why real estate, while inconvenient as money, is more convenient as savings.
13. For a fascinating overview of how various elements would do as money, explaining why gold is uniquely suited for that role, see Planet Money (2011).
14. Sweden used copper as money. Because the metal is quite common, you needed a lot of it to transact. Eventually they were issuing 15 kg lumps of copper as money—surely difficult to carry around.
15. Weatherford (1997).
16. Weber (2014).
17. Thompston's Bank Note and Commercial Reporter in New York, January 1, 1854, cited after Weber (2014).
18. In order to eliminate these costly frictions, US passed National Banking Act that took hold in 1863. The aim of the Act was on-par acceptance of banknotes throughout the country. It was achieved with a clearinghouse operations and insurance schemes.
19. See Katz and Shapiro (1985), Rolfs (1974).
20. See Weatherford (1997).

21. The network effects literature also recognizes "excess momentum," where people adopt a worse technology too early because they expect everyone else to do so as well. But this is unlikely to occur in the context of currency. People tend to be very conservative when it comes to innovations related to money.

22. See Weber (2014).

23. Originally, a piece of silver was worth the same as the equivalent weight of barley. The value of silver was counted in shekels. And the word "shekel" is derived from "weight of barley."

24. In some cases, however, cultural legacy may prevail despite sub-optimality. Several arguments speak to the point that $1 US bill is not optimal, and should be replaced by a coin for durability and cost of handling. See *The Economist* (2013).

25. See Weatherford (1997).

26. The *Oxford English Dictionary* defines one of the meanings of "virtual" as "such in essence, potentiality, or effect, although not in form or actuality."

CHAPTER 3

1. See Gans and Halaburda (2015) and Fung and Halaburda (2014).

2. Notice we are not talking about companies whose main business model is to facilitate payments with regular state-issued currencies, like PayPal, M-Pesa, or the recently emerging Venmo app. The key difference is that these payment platforms do not introduce alternative currencies.

3. See Gans and Halaburda (2015) and Fung and Halaburda (2014).

4. Although, in the United States, under special conditions you can take out a mortgage for such purposes.

5. eBay probably decided to ban such trading to avoid legal suits. Technically, such in-game assets are the property of the game, unless specifically otherwise stated. For example,

in Second Life, another "virtual world," the individuals are the owners of their in-game digital assets. Accordingly, trade of Second Life assets is allowed on eBay.

6. At the time of writing the book, one such example was www.goldah.com.

7. See Vincent (2011).

8. DKPs originated in the game Everquest in 1999, but since then DKPs were also adopted in many other MMORPGs, including World of Warcraft.

9. Kelion (2013).

10. It is still possible to transfer even a currency that was designed to be nontransferable, if the users have a strong incentive to do so. One way is to transfer the entire character, which requires sharing a login and password. But this is much less convenient for both the buyers and the sellers.

11. The platform provides very sophisticated building and scripting tools to allow the creation of extremely complex objects that may interact with each other and with the avatars in a sophisticated way. One could speculate that part of the challenge for Second Life in attracting a large number of users is the complexity of this user interface. The creation of complex objects requires very special skills and hours of work.

12. One of the famous characters of Second Life, also called the "first virtual millionaire" was Anshe Chung, who established a successful operation developing, renting, and trading virtual real estate. She was reported to have earned over $1 million. See Hof (2006).

13. For example, American Apparel opened a showroom, Reuters hired an in-world reporter, and the Swedish embassy opened an office in Second Life.

14. In 2014, over 90 percent of Facebook's almost 12.5 billion revenue came from advertising. The remainder came from "payments and other fees." See Mashable (2015).

15. Initially the transfer could be performed by exchanging Q-coins first into virtual goods or game chips, both of which are transferable. Game chips can then be exchanged

back into Q-coins. In 2007 Tencent banned the exchange of game chips back into Q-coin, under the pressure of regulators. Transfer and exchange of virtual goods is still possible, as is buying Q-coins as a gift, which is directly deposited into the recipient's account.

16. See Fowler and Qin (2007).
17. See Xinhua (2007a).
18. See Xinhua (2007b).
19. This has been shown in economics research in early 2000s, e.g., Rochet and Tirole (2003), Caillaud and Jullien (2001), Caillaud and Jullien (2003).

CHAPTER 4

1. There are many excellent sources explaining technical aspects of Bitcoin, for example, Andreas Antonopoulos (2014).
2. Here we mean the receiver's address for the current transaction. The receiver may have multiple addresses. In principle, he can use a different address for every transaction.
3. The difficulty of the puzzle does not depend on how many transactions there are in the block. Thus, for a miner it is just as costly to add one transaction to the blockchain as it is to add ten.
4. One of Satoshi Nakamoto's purposes, stated in his 2008 white paper, was to assure "one CPU, one vote" rule, as opposed to "one IP address, one vote" rule. Nakamoto worried that one CPU could take over several IP addresses and have more than democratic power.
5. See Alden (2013).
6. There are "safe custody" schemes for private keys—wallets and websites, which you can access with a password, and if you forget the password, by answering a few secret questions.
7. By some estimates, Bitcoin mining between 2009 and 2014 consumed 150,000 mega-watts of electricity—equivalent to keeping Eiffel Tower lit for 260 years. See Clenfield and Alpeyev (2014).

8. See Unenumerated (2005). In the context of traditional currencies, an analogy here would be Spain mining gold and silver in the Americas, dramatically increasing the supply of those metals in Europe and lowering the value of specie.

9. See Vigna and Casey (2015), Lunt (1996), Holland and Cortese (1995), Levy (1994).

10. Why doesn't Bitcoin have "useful" problems as proof-of-work puzzles? In a good proof-of-work puzzle, the solution is hard to find but easy to verify. Typically, the solution to "useful" problems (for example, in science) is also difficult to verify. The challenge is to find such problems that are useful, hard to solve, but easy to verify.

11. The declining economic rewards for mining bitcoin, mentioned above, will have a similar effect. They could make it unattractive for new miners to enter the system or attractive for current miners to exit, making it more likely that one of the remaining miners takes control of over 50 percent of the network. As we explained, this situation will be alleviated if Bitcoin transactions need to be accompanied by higher fees.

12. See Coindesk (2014a).

13. Our simplified analysis considers an economy that runs only on Bitcoin. The argument becomes more involved when the economy has two different currencies, say state-issued money and a cryptocurrency. Still, even in that case the fixed supply of the cryptocurrency is likely to have a deflationary effect: as more people are trying to use the cryptocurrency to affect more transactions, the prices quoted in the cryptocurrency drop, and the exchange rate appreciates, that is, the cryptocurrency becomes worth more units of the state-issued currency.

14. In terms of our identity, keeping the velocity of money constant, if there is more money to go around, but we have an unchanged number of goods, then the prices of these goods need to adjust upward.

15. One advantage of the reduced validation time is that merchants transacting in Litecoin do not need to wait as long

before receiving sufficient confirmation that the transaction was settled. This is an improvement, but arguably, waiting 2.5 versus 10 minutes is not a meaningful difference either for small-value transactions (which would likely be concluded anyway before the official confirmation is issued) or for higher-value trades (the conclusion of which could be delayed until both parties are certain the payment went through, even though it takes 10 minutes or longer). Finally, a technical problem with a shorter validation time is that it increases the likelihood of blockchain forking—that is, two different miners would process their blocks at roughly the same time, leading to two competing versions of blockchain, one of which would be later annulled.

16. Technically, the algorithm draws a random coin whose owner is then allowed to mine the next block, as long as the wallet holding that coin is online at the time. This means that Peercoin users who are holding more coins than others are also have a higher probability of one of their coins being selected and, thus, a higher probability of mining the next block and getting the reward.

17. Luckycoin is a modification of Litecoin with the added feature that randomized the reward for mining a block. The standard reward for each block is 88 luckycoins. However, with a 5 percent probability the miner could get twice as many coins; with a 1 percent probability, five times as many coins; and with a 0.01 percent probability, 58 times as many coins as the reward for mining a new block.

18. See CryptoCoinsNews (2014).

19. The change was announced in April 2014. See https://wiki.reddcoin.com/index.php?title=History_of_Reddcoin.

20. This does not mean that Ripple is always perceived this way by government regulators. In May 2015, FinCEN (the Financial Crimes Enforcement Network, an institution that protects US financial networks from illegal activities) fined Ripple Labs for not registering with FinCEN as a money services business even though Ripple Labs was in the business of exchanging its XRP cryptocurrency for traditional state-issued currencies such as the US dollar.

21. They were developed at the end of 2014 (see Coindesk 2014b) and they are available, for example, in Chicago or in Warsaw, Poland.

22. For accounting purposes, some prices may be posted in a fraction of a penny, but actual transactions are then always rounded up. In the United States, gas prices are often posted at gas stations in tenths of a penny, e.g., $2.879 per gallon. This is because people typically buy many gallons. And even if the total comes up with a fraction, e.g. $31.669 for 11 gallons, it is rounded up to a cent, $31.67. Very small denominations of cash are often not available on principle. Canada is not issuing 1-cent coins anymore, because the value of the materials is larger than the nominal value of the coin. Cash transactions are rounded up to 5 cents. If the register rings CAD $13.22, you pay $13.20. If it rings $13.23, you pay $13.25. Interestingly, transactions with credit or debit cards are still with 1-cent precision.

23. People sometimes argue that Bitcoin is risky because relying on it means putting your trust in an anonymous programmer (or programmers) whose true intentions are unknown. However, Bitcoin requires on the well-known and well-understood cryptographic tools that also underlie much of traditional payment infrastructure, e-commerce, and so on. This means that if we trust the encryption of online banking or retail (as most people do), we should have the same trust in Bitcoin.

24. With credit cards, it is possible that the consumer will challenge the transactions, e.g., because it was made with a stolen credit card number. In such a case, the merchant usually does not get the money, even if he already provided the service or merchandise.

25. In the early 2000s, both HD DVD and Blu-ray looked like viable formats for high definition DVD systems. But the understanding of the market was that only one format would win—due to the logic of network effects. Many consumers were waiting to buy HD DVD or Blu-ray players until they could see in which format most movies were released. Eventually Blu-ray won the formats war, but its

success in the market was limited. This is because, in the meantime, the popularity of Internet streaming of high-definition movies removed the need to purchase the player altogether.

26. Depending on the merchant's agreement with the credit card acquirer bank, it may take between one and a few days for the money charged with a credit card to be available on the merchants account. Moreover, fees of a few percent are common. An additional benefit of bitcoin for the merchants is the irreversibility of transactions.

27. It is doubtful whether consulting a Bitcoin wallet on the phone takes less time than swiping a card does, even though sending a Bitcoin transaction from a well-designed wallet may be quicker than typing up the credit card information in the case of online transactions. Moreover, credit cards often offer rewards to the customer that bitcoin transactions do not.

References

Alden, William (2013), "The Bitcoin Mines of Iceland," *New York Times*, December 23, http://dealbook.nytimes.com/2013/12/23/morning-agenda-the-bitcoin-mines-of-iceland/?_r=0.

Antonopoulos, Andreas (2014), *Mastering Bitcoin*, O'Reilly Media.

Caillaud, Bernard and Bruno Jullien (2001), "Competing Cybermediaries," *European Economic Review*, 45: 797–808.

Caillaud, Bernard and Bruno Jullien (2003), "Chicken & Egg: Competition among Intermediation Service Providers," *RAND Journal of Economics*, 34: 309–328.

Casadesus-Masanell, Ramon and Feng Zhu (2010), "Strategies to Fight Ad-Sponsored Rivals," *Management Science*, 56: 1484–1499.

Castronova, Edward (2014), *Wildcat Currency*, Yale University Press.

CryptoCoinsNews (2014), "Facebook Approves Dogecoin Tipping App," https://www.cryptocoinsnews.com/facebook-approves-dogecoin-tipping-app/.

Clenfield, Jason and Pavel Alpeyev (2014), "The Other Bitcoin Power Struggle," BusinessWeek, April 24.

Coindesk (2014a), "Are 51% Attacks a Real Threat to Bitcoin?" http://www.coindesk.com/51-attacks-real-threat-bitcoin/.

Coindesk (2014b), "BitOcean Releases Two-Way Bitcoin ATM to Compete with Market Leaders," http://www.coindesk.com/bitocean-releases-two-way-kiosks-compete-bitcoin-atm-market-leaders/.

Comparette, T. Louis (1914), "Debasement of the Silver Coinage under the Emperor Nero," *The American Journal of Numismatics*, 47: 1–11.

The Economist (2013), "Kill bill," March 16, http://www .economist.com/node/21573582/print.

Einzig, Paul (1966), *Primitive Money: In Its Ethnological, Historical and Economical Aspects*, Pergamon.

Evans, David S. (2012), "Facebook Credits: Do Payments Firms Need to Worry," PYMNTS.com, February 28, http://www .pymnts.com/briefing-room/commerce-3-0/facebook -commerce-2/Facebook-Credits-Do-Payments-Firms-Need -to-Worry-2/.

Evans, David S. and Richard Schmalensee (2005), *Paying with Plastic*, MIT Press.

Farrell, Joseph and Garth Saloner (1985), "Standardization, Compatibility, and Innovation," *RAND Journal of Economics*, 16: 70–83.

Fergusson, Niall (2008), *The Ascent of Money*, Penguin Press.

Fowler, Geoffrey A. and Juying Qin (2007), "QQ: China's New Coin of the Realm? Officials Try to Crack Down as Fake Online Currency Is Traded for Real Money," *Wall Street Journal*, March 30.

Fung, Ben and Hanna Halaburda (2014), "Understanding Platform-Based Digital Currencies," *Bank of Canada Review*, Spring: 12–20.

Gandal, Neil and Hanna Halaburda (2014), "Competition in the Cryptocurrency Market," London, Center for Economic Policy Research.

Gans, Joshua and Hanna Halaburda (2015), "Some Economics of Private Digital Currency," *Economic Analysis of the Digital Economy*, A. Goldfarb, S. Greenstein, and C. Tucker (eds.), University of Chicago Press.

Harari, Yuval Noah (2015), *Sapiens: A Brief History of Humankind*, Harper.

Hof, Rob (2006), "Second Life's First Millionaire," BusinessWeek, November 26, http://www.businessweek.com/ the_thread/techbeat/archives/2006/11/second_lifes_fi .html.

Holland, Kelley and Amy Cortese (1995), "The Future of Money," *BusinessWeek*, June 12, http://www.businessweek .com/1995/24/b3428001.htm.

Jevons, William Stanley (1875), *Money and the Mechanism of Exchange*, Macmillan.

Katz, Michael L. and Carl Shapiro (1985), "Network Externalities, Competition, and Compatibility," *American Economic Review*, 75: 424–440.

Kelion, Leo (2013), "Diablo 3 auction houses are doomed by developer Blizzard," BBC News Technology, September 18, http://www.bbc.com/news/technology-24152225.

Kiyotaki, Nobuhiro and Randall Wright (1989), "On Money as a Medium of Exchange," *Journal of Political Economy*, 97: 927–954.

Levy, Steven (1994), "E-Money (That's What I Want)," *Wired*, December 1, http://archive.wired.com/wired/archive/ 2.12 /emoney_pr.html.

Lunt, Penny (1996), "E-cash becomes reality, via Mark Twain and Digicash," ABA Banking Journal, 88: 62.

Martin, Felix (2014), *Money: The Unauthorized Biography*, Knopf.

Mashable (2015), "Facebook's annual revenue topped $10 billion for the first time in 2014," January 28, http://mash able.com/2015/01/28/facebook-q4-earnings-2014/.

Nakamoto, Satoshi (2008), "Bitcoin: A Peer-to-Peer Electronic Cash System," https://bitcoin.org/bitcoin.pdf.

Pagliery, Jose (2014), *Bitcoin and the Future of Money*, Triumph Books.

Planet Money (2011), "A Chemist Explains Why Gold Beat Out Lithum, Osmium, Einstainium . . ." http://www.npr .org/blogs/money/2011/02/15/131430755/a-chemist -explains-why-gold-beat-out-lithium-osmium-einsteinium.

Rochet, Jean-Charles and Jean Tirole (2002), "Cooperation among Competitors: Some Economics of Payment Card Associations," *RAND Journal of Economics*, 33: 549–570.

Rochet, Jean-Charles and Jean Tirole (2003), "Platform Competition in Two-Sided Markets," *Journal of the European Economic Association*, 1: 990–1029.

Rohlfs, Jeffrey (1974), "A Theory of Interdependent Demand for a Communications Service," *Bell Journal of Economics and Management Science*, 5: 16–37.

Sargent, Thomas J. and Francois R. Velde (2002), *The Big Problem of Small Change*, Princeton University Press.

Sheck, Justin (2008), "Mackerel Economics in Prison Leads to Appreciation for Oily Fillets," *Wall Street Journal*, October 2, http://www.wsj.com/articles/SB122290720439096481.

Tschoegl, Adrian E. (2001) "Maria Theresa's Thaler: A Case of International Money," *Eastern Economic Journal*, 27: 445–464.

Unenumerated (2005), *Bit gold*, http://unenumerated.blogs pot.ca/2005/12/bit-gold.html.

Vigna, Paul and Michael J. Casey (2015), *The Age of Cryptocurrency*, St. Martin's Press.

Vincent, Danny (2011), "China Used Prisoners in Lucrative Gaming Work," *The Guardian*, May 25, http://www.theguardian.com/world/2011/may/25/china-prisoners-internet-gaming-scam.

Weatherford, Jack (1997), *The History of Money*, Three Rivers Press.

Weber, Warren E. (2014), "The Efficiency of Private E-Money Like Systems: The US Experience with State Bank Notes," Bank of Canada Working Paper No. 2014–15.

Xinhua (2007a), "Central Bank alert on 'virtual money,'" http://en.people.cn/200701/12/eng20070112_340681.html.

Xinhua (2007b), "Virtual currency requires tough new regula tions," http://news.xinhuanet.com/english/2007-02/12/content_5730970.htm.

Yglesias, Matthew (2012), "Social Cash: Could Facebook Credits Ever Compete with Dollars and Euros?" *Slate*, February 29, http://www.slate.com/articles/business/cashless_society/2012/02/facebook_credits_how_the_social_network_s_currency_could_compete_with_dollars_and_euros_.htm.

INDEX

CPSIA information can be obtained
at www.ICGtesting.com
Printed in the USA
LVHW05*1357290418
575310LV00009B/521/P